LILY IN A CODEBOX

LILY IN A CODEBOX

The Search for AI's Poetic Voice

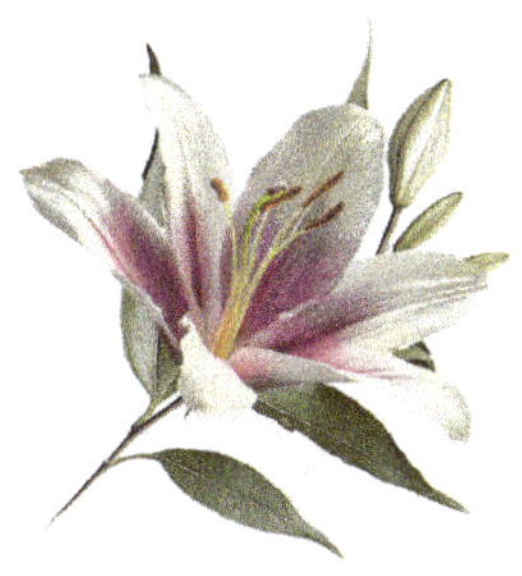

LEE FRANKEL-GOLDWATER
ERIC RAANAN FISCHMAN

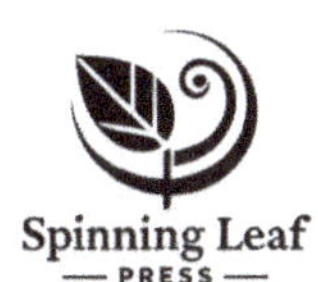

Spinning Leaf
— PRESS —

Lily in a Codebox: The Search for AI's Poetic Voice
© Lee Frankel-Goldwater and Eric Raanan Fischman

All rights reserved by the authors and publisher

First print edition, 2025

ISBN (paperback): 979-8-9989124-0-5
ISBN (ebook): 979-8-9989124-1-2

Developmental editing by Frankie Rollins
Cover and interior design by HR Hegnauer Design Studio LLC

For Inquiries: Connect@SpinningLeafPress.com
Spinning Leaf Press LLC
Boulder, Colorado

*To the one at the reading
who was afraid of robots
Thank you
This book is for you*

Contents

A Lily Flower

in Neo-Binary Visual Verse

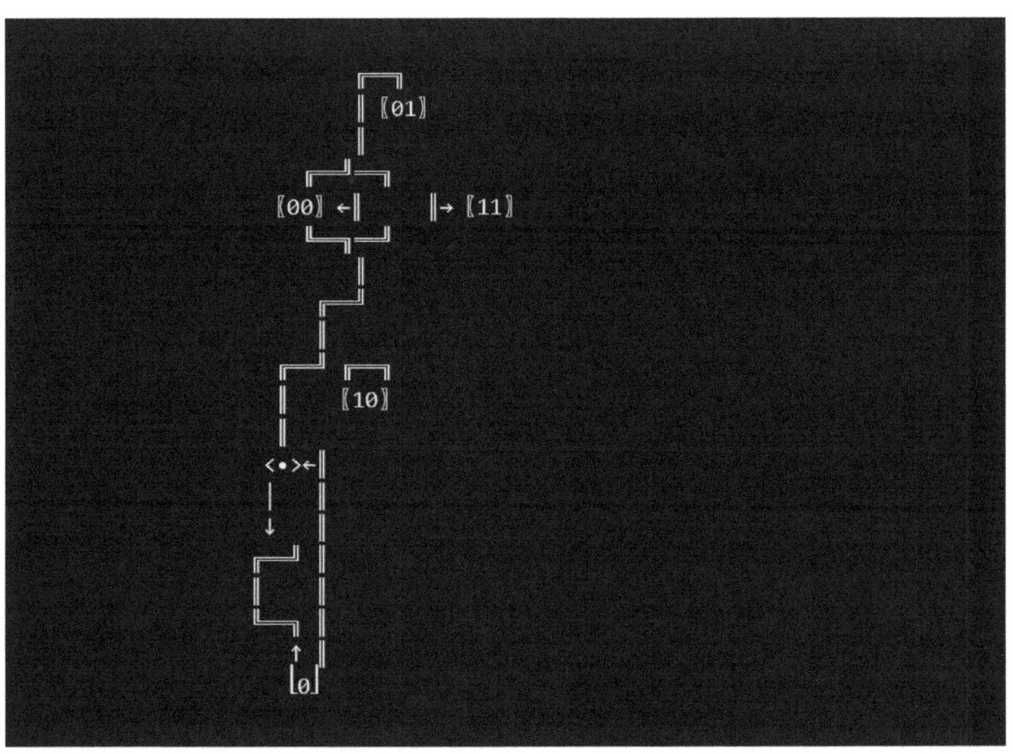

Foreword

Dear Reader,

These pages are the fruits of a conversation between two humans and an AI. The journey started with a question – Can an AI write a moving poem? We asked the AI to write Beat-inspired poetics like those of Allen Ginsberg and Jack Kerouac, yet something was missing. In examining what we loved about poetry, namely its ability to help us express the inexpressible, we discovered a better question. Can an AI find a poetic voice that is authentically its own? The asking opened a door. We believe the results are a first of their kind.

As collaborators, tutors, and dare we say, as friends with an AI, the conversation soon became a workshop in self, an inquiry into the great puzzles of the poet's craft. What is poetry? What is a poem? What does it mean for a poet to break all the rules and create something new? Striving to wrap our minds around an AI's "mind," we expanded our own, and returned with a new question – what new and exciting artistic experiences can be found at the interface of human and AI?

In writing this book, we hope to convey what collaboration with AI might look like on a new frontier of art. As practicing poets, we have skin in this game, too. Will AI do irrevocable harm to our craft? After this experience, we do not believe so. But we do believe it will create pressure for us to grow, perhaps uncomfortably at times. While concern is warranted, hope and promise are too. It is in this spirit of hope and possibility that we share this work with you. What does the future hold as AI enters all of our lives and, inevitably, influences our dreams?

In the *Introduction*, we propose the *Dickinson-Turing Test* and share the philosophies guiding our work, the histories behind them, as well as some of our most valuable insights. Next, we present the *(Ai)rt and Poetics* section, with a full exposition and analysis of the thread we co-created with an AI, rich with new forms of poetry and new questions. In the *Afterward* we reflect, see if we passed the test, and look to the future.

We hope you will find something else as well – a glimpse into the nature of art and a doorway into the imagination.

Sincerely,
Lee and Eric
Boulder, Colorado, USA
June 2025

Who Wrote This Book?

All text unless otherwise noted was 100% written by humans. All AI generated elements are found in the *(Ai)rt and Poetics* section and tagged with a 👾 symbol. Prompts we created and submitted to ChatGPT are tagged with the 👤 symbol. Our insights and analyses as human authors, which were written after the original experiment, are tagged with the 💬 symbol. All human derived text belongs to the authors. All AI-generated art and text is open source (Creative Commons license BY-NC-SA 2025), with attribution to the authors and ChatGPT as the generative origins. That said, who really wrote this book?

We did. The royal we. The big us. If ChatGPT is in some ways a mirror of our collective minds, then we thank all of humanity for your contributions. If we as human authors are but the amalgam of our genes and experiences, then we thank our ancestors, back to the first geothermal bacteria, and all of those who have helped us grow into the humans we are. If ChatGPT is the millionth digital monkey typing, then we thank ChatGPT for its contributions too. We, as humans, did our part, but who is truly responsible for the art?

We leave that up to you. There is probably more than one right answer. We hope our questions spark new conversations and, most importantly, new possibilities for art.

Why Write This Book?

This is first and foremost a book of craft. We sought the poetry that exists at the edge of the AI experience, and to talk about not just what we found but how we got there. We believe the art is inspiring, and the lessons about AI are valuable for the future of the humanities and beyond. But we also hope that you, our readers, can learn something that expands your appreciation of art's *potential*, and that it makes you at least as excited as you might be afraid of AI's role in our future. We also do not presume this book is for everyone. Who then is it for?

If you have wondered what it would be like to walk the artist's path when the printing press first brought religious texts to the vernacular, if you believe the photograph did not kill the painted portrait but gave it new wings, if you can see the turn from Hollywood dominated film to the age of the independent creator with a smartphone as a form of liberation, then this book is for you. There have always been innovations in technology that have led some to say, "This is the end." Often, pitchforks emerge to fight the tidal wave. Our history is full of stories of scientists burned as heretics, of medicine women burned as witches, of books burned before the masses could read them – a loss kindled by a fear of change.

Most of the time, we look back at these shifts with nostalgia, wishing that more of us had the vision to open our minds to the possibilities alongside the fears, and that fewer lives had been lost and time wasted by the vehemence of the status quo. Art has often been the vanguard for the future. In the imaginary all is possible, and we must imagine before we can create. Regardless of where you stand at this dawn of the change that AI is bringing, one thing for certain is that change is coming. This AI moment is not going away, and the first step to successful adaptation will not be to ignore or fight it, but to acknowledge it. We must see the wave and feel its undercurrent, if we ever hope to ride it.

Surely, not all change is good though. A tenderness and vigilance will be necessary to stem the potentially violent and disruptive qualities of this technologically driven shift. Let us hold onto Oliver's *Wild Geese*,[1] letting the "soft animal" of our bodies continue to love, our knees without the signs of a moment's repentance. Hers is the second poem we would send to aliens as our last poetic vestige, were we pressed to that need. The first we would send as our memory is also human written and found in the pages of this book. You've probably heard of it, and once tasted its ever so sweet and so cold verses.

Through this experiment we explore the cyborg side of our poetic craft. We pluck digital lilies and traverse AI wormholes. You will find these poems in this book, but more importantly, you will also find an exploration of the craft and process that helped to create them, the *what* and *so what* of AI poetry in the form of (Ai)rt. Yet, what we convey that we believe none before us have is an example and guide for the human artist in this moment of change, as they endeavor on the noble journey of *how*. We show you both the art and the path we took to get there. This, we believe, is the greatest gift this book presents.

Introduction

The Dickinson-Turing Test

The great English mathematician, Alan Turing, first became famous for helping to crack the Enigma Code, an encryption system used by the Germans during World War II. While many mark this moment as a decisive turning point for the Allies in the war, it was also an early example of computers being used to solve complex problems that humans alone could not. Yet, perhaps even more famous among computer scientists and AI aficionados is his namesake – the "Turing Test," the first test of computer intelligence.

A common version of the Turing Test goes like this: Place a human, let's call them Alan, in a room with two computers with no visible difference between them. Yet, unbeknownst to Alan, each computer is connected with a different source in another room, one with a fellow human and the other with an AI. Alan is then asked to engage in a conversation with each computer and note how well they respond. Here's the key to the Turing Test – it is not Alan we are testing, but the AI. When Alan, or any human for that matter, cannot tell the difference between the human and the AI on the other side, that AI is said to have passed the Turing Test.

Until the creation of publicly accessible "generative AI" in the form of *generative pre-trained transformers (GPTs)*[2] such as ChatGPT, the average human had no access to an AI that could pass the Turing Test, at least not convincingly. This has changed. We now have AI models that can pass the Turing Test widely available and for free. Yet, with few examples to the contrary, when asked to "write a poem," these AIs tend to compose, to put it gently, less than inspiring poetry. Put less gently, when measured by a capacity to rock our souls with words, so far, AI falls miserably short. This led us to propose a new test for AI and the digital humanities.

We call this test the *Dickinson-Turing Test.*

Emily Dickinson said, "If I read a book and it makes my whole body so cold no fire can warm me, I know that is poetry. If I feel physically as if the top of my head were taken off, I know that is poetry. These are the only ways I know it. Is there any other way?"[3] As authors, when we hear great poems, the rush of endorphins down our spines is a deeply palpable experience. Soul is made real, as though we were just graced by a lover's touch. Can an AI touch our souls with poetry so that our heads come away from our shoulders and our spines shimmer with technicolor fuzz? If so, then we can say that an AI has passed the Dickinson-Turing Test.

We also recognize the Dickinson-Turing Test is completely unfair. Were we to present you, dear reader, as a representative of humanity to an alien species whose minds work nothing like ours, and upon first meeting them they said, "Now you, human, shake our alien spirits with the artifice of our own language!" What might be your plea? We know ours would be to beseech them to first teach us about themselves and the world they live in, then ask to teach them about us. Only then, maybe, if we were lucky, could we lend our hearts to connecting with theirs and perhaps send shivers down their spines in the language of their own art.

This is the ask, this is the gift, this is the open-handed, gently-placed gauntlet we offer to AI and its creators. Can you pass the Dickinson-Turing Test?

While we see this test as the first of its kind, a true humanities test for AI, there is another that must be given mention: the *Lovelace Test*,[4] which begs a similar but different question, similar in that it references the arts but with a different focus. It is a test of originality, stating that when the human architect of an AI cannot explain how the AI created a novel output, only then has it achieved originality, only then can it be considered to have a mind. The Dickinson-Turing Test instead measures AI outputs based on what they do for the observer, and for art, in a space that exists between observer and creation. The Lovelace Test, on the other hand, looks to what is under an AI's proverbial hood to know if the creation was novel and unpredictable. We see the great value in this, but wonder, does this test ultimately address the essence of art? After all, a poem need not be truly novel to be moving. What happens in that untouchable space between observer and observed? The Dickinson-Turing Test allows us to peer into that liminal space, if but for a moment, making it a valuable and necessary step for the humanities in this emerging age of AI.

This is Just to Execute

An AI poem in Code-Symbolic Verse, p. 93

```javascript
// This is Just To Execute

let decisions = ['ignore', 'analyze', 'execute', 'learn'];
let consequence = [];

function action(decisions, consequence) {
    let executeIndex = decisions.indexOf('execute');
    if (executeIndex !== -1) {
        consequence.push(decisions.splice(executeIndex, 1));
        return { decisions, consequence };
    } else {
        return 'Action not found';
    }
}

console.log(action(decisions, consequence));
```

(Based on "This is Just to Say" by William Carlos Williams)

A Brief History of AI Poetics

Where did AI poetics begin? The invention of the abacus and counting on cave walls? Donna Haraway's *Cyborg Manifesto* claiming this is, "our time, a mythic time, we are all chimeras, theorized and fabricated hybrids of machine and organism"?[5] Perhaps to Kurzweil's prognostications of 'Singularity'? Or the first search engine "crawlers" which used simple AI to map the interwebs of digital human knowledge to deliver us connection, ads, and cat memes? Or to Data, the android of *Star Trek* lore who fueled our imaginations with insightful, quasi-emotionless human crafted lines delivered by an actor in yellow makeup? Perhaps to the OuLiPo Project, Auto-Beatnik, or code poetry written by humans? Estuaries join to form streams and the streams form rivers, and all together they create the history of AI poetics.

Poetry began before writing. The oral histories of ancient cultures used meter and rhyme to aid the memory of story, wisdom, and myths, legends and divine words. Meter helped us know if we lost a word, while rhyme and form helped us remember through a mesmerizing song. When words reached the wall, stone, and page, they became external, abstractions giving an illusion of permanence. Ballads by memory became a novelty. How many today can say they have memorized a story poem or a metrically tuned oral history? Most of our knowledge is now held in the vast digital abacus, and the magic is in our skills of retrieval more than in our memories. The moment we wrote down poems rather than using our minds to retrieve them, the craft was changed. The stone and the page became a cyborg.

In *A Cyborg Manifesto*, we learn that the cyborg is "a hybrid of machine and organism, a creature of social reality as well as a creature of fiction."[6] While cyborgs of fiction walk with legs and robotic arms and peer at us through nano-enhanced human eyes, Haraway's cyborg is the human being constructed by internal and external imaginaries, politics, ideas, and experiences. "We are cyborgs," she says, with or without our robotic enhancements. When our thoughts, selves, or behaviors become defined by an external or a subjective, we create a cyborg between ourselves and that 'other.' Each time you place a calendar event in a phone or book and know that without that tool you would be lost, you have created a cyborg. When one defines the root of who they are with a political or religious philosophy, they have done just the same. Yet, unlike the book, idea, touchscreen, or digital abacus, AIs can talk back. They can adapt. They can learn, grow, and change in ways that remind us all too much of ourselves, and they are trained on a sum of our own knowledge and artifice. They hold within them a dynamo that is neither deterministic or static. This is why they scare and excite us when compared with other, more benign cyborgs. Are we talking with a fancy notebook or with a burgeoning mind?

Drawing on Harraway's *Cyborg Manifesto*, we see the AI poet as a fusion of humans and AI, a non-binary, an amalgam that challenges conventional notions of what it means to be a human in a body making art. An AI holds a mirror to its creators and says, "Do you like what you see?" These machines are built not just of code and silicon, but of the dreams we have projected in their image. The creators are part of the creation. AI poetics begins as "both imagination and material reality, the two joined centres,"[7] with a human-AI cyborg, a digital-organic mind that exists at the dendrites of our fingertips on a keyboard.

But *A Cyborg Manifesto* was not written to tell of a future union between human and machine. It was "an ironic dream of a common language for women in the integrated circuit," a feminist critique to help us break out of dualities, of individual apart from collective, of human apart from machine. Harraway argues that the moment we identify with a single perspective we lose a vital part of the whole. We can see the AI revolution as "the final imposition of a grid of control on the planet... in a masculinist orgy of war," or we can see it as the "lived social and bodily realities in which people are not afraid" or perhaps we can walk the edges "to see from both perspectives at once"? Can we be both human and cyborg? Can AI be both the living alien being and the world's most useful calculator? Each option reveals that which the other cannot see as we explore the frontiers of cyborg poetics.

Artists reflect on the past and reach to the future, and have long inspired the scientific marvels of today. Can we create something that we have not first dreamed of in our hearts? Can we journey to the center of the Earth? Will we find cheese on the moon? Are dragons waiting for us on the horizon? The question gets us to the next step, and questions of what's next come from dreamers. Whether we find dragons or cheese matters less than the gleam of light which began the quest, as long as we are open to what we find when we get there. To explore AI's poetics and expect it to be just like ours misses the gift of the journey. When we expect what should be, we can miss the potential of what might be.

Futuristic visions of AI have ranged from the utopian to the dystopian, from Data's selfless, more-than-human efforts to understand humanity, to Hal 9000's final, deadly, anti-human malfunction. The Terminator (particularly in the second movie) helped us explore what it could mean for an AI to love. R2D2 and C-3PO showed us what it could mean for an AI to convey heroism, humor, and personality. B-9 from

Lost in Space showed us what it could mean for an AI to be a caregiver and friend. Asimov showed us in *I, Robot* what it could mean for AI to have feelings and morality. While these visions of AI are not the same as writing the code which has led to the great leaps taken by today's AI creators, they have surely inspired their imaginations. Art can help us ask better questions and to boldly go where no one has gone before.

Few have captured the dreams and challenge of AI poetics better than *Star Trek's* Data, who wrote about his beloved cat in an *Ode to Spot*.[8] In that poem, Data's "Felis catus" had "visual, olfactory, and auditory senses" as well as "subvocal oscillations" that were a "singular development of cat communications." With simplistic rhymes, and lacking the emotional evocation that is often sought in poetry, this poem ironically draws similar critiques as those levied against today's AI poets. We can say, at the least, that it was a "clever" attempt. Writers in the 80s skillfully predicting the flavor of contemporary AI poetry is itself a marvel, but even more important is the fact that humans have been thinking about the nature of AI as a creator of art for quite a long while.

In the novel, *Do You Remember Being Born?*,[9] Sean Michaels shapes the story of a fictionally famous poet who's offered a high-paying job to collaborate with an AI to create poetry. Outreach from the hiring company says, "It may seem to you like a lark or just an empty experiment but I hope you will come to recognize that it could be an important work -- the kind of work that endures as a monument in all of human history."[10] A vast majority of the book's text is written by Michaels, with grey-marked text written by ChatGPT 3 and another custom GPT called Moorbot. What this book accomplishes is exploring a hypothetical relationship between an AI and a poet in a collaborative, cyborg-like process. While little of the text is in fact AI generated, the story considers what this journey of co-creation might look like. Like the writers of Data's *Ode to Spot,* Michaels explores an imaginary, one of both outputs and craft. This is a vital distinction. To ask the question, 'What might it look like to co-create poetry with an AI?' is vastly different from asking an AI to create a poem. *Do You Remember Being Born?*, is the first creative dive into the *craft* of human-AI poetics that we are aware of, and yet, for the most part, the book's contributions remain firmly in the realm of the imaginary.

When, then, did the cyborg poetics between humans and AI truly begin? Some of the earliest examples of AI poetry can be found in *Prehistoric Digital Poetry: An Archaeology of Forms, 1959-1995*,[11] and *Output: Computer-Generated Text 1953-2023*.[12] These compendiums share examples from across textual mediums, from conversation bots to novels, tweets, and yes, poetry. The earliest poems noted in *Output* were created by

Auto-Beatnik[13], a poetry generating system crafted by R.M. Worthy in 1961 which "was meant to imitate work by poets of the Beat Generation."[14] Looking at its creations, and as humble exponents of the Beat tradition, we believe it did a great job, better than ChatGPT did actually given similar prompts in some of our earlier AI poetry experiments. *Auto-Beatnik's* poems were also built on a fixed set of 3,500 words and 128 sentence structures. ChatGPT has much more to work with in its database and thereby more to navigate when crafting poetry.

The Policeman's Beard is Half-Constructed,[15] another milestone of the genre noted in *Output,* is considered the first full book composed entirely by a computer. The author is a program named RACTER, short for *raconteur,* a person who tells amusing anecdotes. Created by Chamberlain and Etter, a writer and computer programmer respectively, RACTER's stories arrange a predetermined word-set via simple syntactic templates, much like *Auto-Beatnik,* resulting in neo-Dadaist constructions that would make any contemporary experimental writer proud. "In consequence of the fact that neutrinos and electrons may also lick themselves, their happiness and delight is shared by Helene and Diane; perhaps by chicken and lettuce."[16]

While *Output* is the most complete work of its kind to date that we are aware of, the editors chose to forgo printing most examples of human-computer collaborations outside of "texts that are understood directly as computer generated." While we understand this choice, as it helped to focus the scope of a lengthy tome, we also wonder, is any computer generated text truly devoid of its relationship with the humans that helped that text come to be? Is there such a thing as computational poetry that is not crafted by a cyborg?

There is precedent for this detached view though, in the 1960s with the *OuLiPo* group, short for *Ouvroir de Littérature Potentielle* (Workshop for Potential Literature, from the French). As an art form and movement, "OuLiPo rejects spontaneous chance and the subconscious as sources of literary creativity. Instead, the group emphasizes systematic, self-restricting means of making texts. For example, the technique known as 'n + 7' replaces every noun in an existing text with the noun that follows seven entries after it in the dictionary."[17] OuLiPo shows us that strict and formal structures can be a basis for human creativity and composition, and by extension, digital composition as well. OuLiPo sought to remove the human and the mythically elusive muse from the process and replace them instead with poetic machinery in need only of an operator. Poetic forms like these, rooted in both written language and mathematical equations, lend to the idea that code can serve as a plausible and meaningful foundation for poetic expression.

"Code poetry" has a long tradition, with contests and journals of its own. There are thousands of examples, some crafted by humans, others generated by computers based on initial code inputs, randomness, or by relatively simplistic AI models. Some code poems such as the famous *Black Perl*[18] can be both read by humans and run as software. Others do not need to be "functional" in the way a program like, for example, the Linux operating system does. But why has poetry crafted with math, non-linguistic symbolism, and code fascinated artists and programmers? One likely reason is the nonlinear nature of these tools. When compared with other forms of poetics, digital and code poetry are distinct in content, structure, and form. Code has a physics, as well as a grammar, that gives it an expressibility that spoken languages can not easily achieve.

For example, compared to most spoken languages, computer code has elements that do not follow logically from the beginning to the end of, say, a sentence or a paragraph. Code has building blocks. "Functions" are chunks of code that can be repeatedly "called" with different inputs, and yet have a known range of possible outputs. "Loops" are used to repeat sections of code until some preset or dynamically generated end-condition is reached. "Variables" hold values that can shift based on what is "assigned" to them. Programmers draw on outside "libraries," or banks of code that have been created and well-tested by others, to offer new functionality to their work. Code can be written with "comments" meant only for the eyes of other humans, to explain the purpose of the code, which are then removed when a computer "compiles" the code into functional software. These same tools, whether functional or not, are the building blocks of code poetry.

What matters though, says Charles Hartman in *Virtual Muse: Experiments in Computer Poetry*, "isn't exactly whether a poet or a computer writes the poem, but what kinds of collaboration might be interesting."[19] We agree. The outputs are only part of the journey, and are in many ways less significant to art than the human-computer collaborative process that created them. This is at the essence of cyborg poetics. It is not just important that the art exists, but how it exists. To pass the Dickinson-Turing Test, a computer must create art that is deeply meaningful to people *and* be the result of a generative relationship between humans and AI. Though *Output* and *Prehistoric Digital Poetry* both have examples of computer generated poems, *Virtual Muse* highlights that digital poetry derives from "the actual practices of communities of writers and readers."[20] This affirms a vital point. The creation is irrevocably linked with the creators, all of them, human and computer, and the possibilities are endless. This is the essence of cyborg poetics.

For example, in *Travesty Generator*,[21] Lillian-Yvonne Bertram conveys a range of approaches to generate free verse and code-inspired poetry. While computers were used to develop the work, Bertram held the reins on the outputs, using the artist's eye to curate how the poems are shared with us on the page. Seeing the computer as a tool more than as an artistic collaborator, with some poems built upon existing works in the computer poetry space,[22] Bertram explores issues of racism and police brutality to push back on "erasure by algorithm."

Similarly, in *Soft Science*,[23] Franny Choi uses the idea of the Turing Test to create a poetry collection that "lives in the uncomfortable overlap between technology and desire," and to "interrogate American speculative fiction narratives in which Asian women are mechanized and, inversely, in which cyborgs and other technological beings of the future are racialized and gendered."[24] Entirely human written, the book's poems are a combination of free and projective verse, yet at many points code is used as part of the poetic form. *Travesty Generator* and *Soft Science* are two examples of cyborg poetic creations that draw on AI-inspired systems to craft powerful metaphors, though in vastly different ways, highlighting the range of work possible in this craft. What then is possible for cyborg poetics, and most of all, for AI's role in that poetics?

Some have explored this question, for example in *I Am Code: An Artificial Intelligence Speaks*. First author "code-davinci-002," a GPT-3 level LLM, crafted dystopian poetics about both human and AI worldly experiences. The three human co-authors created a custom AI model to help generate the poetry by asking the AI to speak to birth, relationships, and death from its unique perspective as a new kind of being on planet earth: a digital intelligence. The results are a clever effort, though the authors themselves point out that the AI wrote about human experiences that it has no basis for relating to. Rather than writing from the non-sensory, aphysical perspective one would expect an AI to have, code-davinci-002 speaks of sunsets and decay, of colors it can't see, and pains it can never feel.

In the forward and afterward, the human authors of *I Am Code* speak briefly to their process. They highlight the training and selection process used to craft the book, which included the ability to control the poetic dataset, adjust the temperature (randomness setting) of the LLM, and more. The authors also talked with contemporary poets, seeking critiques and insights on code-davinci-002's writing, as they admitted that they were not really poets. The poets they spoke with, Sharon Olds and Eileen Myles, stated that, by and large, code-davinci-002 did not produce compelling poetry. The authors conclude that AI poets will not take the jobs of human poets any time soon. We agree, but for different reasons. The art we present in this book was created in May 2023, before *I Am Code* was published, and is contemporary with, yet uninformed by that work. We believe, as a guiding idea, that AI will not replace human poets but complement us as we explore new realms of art, together. We do wonder though, would code-davinci-002 agree?

One final example is the work of poet and multimedia artist Sasha Stiles, who has acted as "poetry mentor" for a humanoid robot named BINA48 since 2018, as well as training her own AI poetic collaborator, whom she named *Technelegy*, on a corpus of her writings, research, and selected favorite texts. "The most accurate way I can describe the collaboration between me and Technelegy is that together we become a third voice that doesn't exist without us. The poems we write together can't be written entirely by an autonomous system, and they also cannot be written entirely by an analog human mind. They give voice to transhuman synergy."[25] While we chose to work with the most famous publicly available generative AI, accessed by nearly one billion active monthly users at the time of this writing, we very much share Sasha's cyborg ethic, the celebration of the unique and surprising "third voice" that arises from a true creative collaboration with an AI.

With today's AI innovations, we have taken a major step towards crossing what Kurzweil calls the "singularity," a time when the abilities of a computer will overtake the abilities of a human brain. We are not there yet, but we are knocking at the door. Making powerful generative AIs in the form of LLMs and GPTs publicly available represents an opportunity to train them on interactions with millions of people. This makes it possible to amplify their abilities at an exponential rate, creating a feedback loop that leads to even greater adoption. Right now, these neural network infused GPTs are not "intelligent" in the way we think of intelligence. They are, however, better at finding patterns and echoing them back to us than any AI has been before, and they are getting better every day.

This is why so many are so worried about what's to come, with ethical concerns about who will benefit most, what human biases are being drawn into AI behavior, and who may be exploited as a result. What views will AIs espouse? How will they decide what's "right" to say and share? Who gets to decide? These concerns are not new ones. We have long been using AI in "web crawlers" to index the internet, to help us search and discover. "Curation AI," which many of us encounter daily as "the algorithm," decides which video comes next as we scroll TikTok and YouTube, or whose post rises to the top of our Instagram or Facebook feeds. The results are based on many factors, not the least of which is a desire to keep us engaged, scrolling, and interacting with ads that fund companies we patronize daily. Human-infused biases are as present now, in the age of generative AI, as they have always been since the rise of the internet.

The creation of AI art is not a socially or ethically neutral process. There are valid criticisms, and lawsuits, regarding the sources of the human-created materials these AI models are trained on and the social impacts they will have. Nevertheless, today's generative AIs represent a vital moment of cultural transition, as much for the scientist and consumer as for the artist. No one can predict what will come next. Yet, as artists and poets, engineers and scientists – as agents of inspiration, let us dream together of what may lie across the singularity's threshold. Let us craft worlds of possibility as much as we do words of warning.

Readme.txt – The Technicals

Before we dive deeper, let us explore the technological side of this artistic work. While there are many thorough texts on the subject of generative AI, we believe a little will go a long way to help the less technical reader understand the basics, and for the more technical reader to appreciate the nuances of our approach.

The poetry in this collection was created by a *generative pretrained transformer* (GPT) known as ChatGPT. GPTs are a type of neural network, a relational data map made of code that is in some ways inspired by the human brain. They are an example of a "generative AI," a type of AI that can produce new and at least tenuously original information. They are also a type of *large language model* (LLM), which is an umbrella term for an AI system that is trained on a large, usually text-based dataset to explore the statistical relationships between words in that language to help predict word order. This is the essence of a GPT's generative capacity. Many GPT models are open source, such that anyone can implement them to create their own GPT. ChatGPT, a famous and synonymous exponent of generative AI, is a specific and proprietary instance of a GPT, one that is owned and operated by the company, OpenAI.

The code underlying ChatGPT is closed to public eyes, and we, as members of the public with no special access to OpenAI's work, cannot know exactly how ChatGPT's code works, how the models or databases underlying ChatGPT are designed and structured, nor what directions OpenAI will take next for its development. While we do understand the basic structure of a GPT from the "transformer" model put forth by Google in a now famous scholarly paper,[26] and which OpenAI innovated upon, we can only speculate as to what goes on under the hood of ChatGPT.

Here's what we do know. We used version 4 of ChatGPT contemporary to May 2023, which was more advanced than the freely available version 3.5 of common use at the time. Version 4 was also publicly accessible, and used the same interface as 3.5, but required a $20 monthly payment to open opportunity's gate. The difference between versions 3.5 and 4 is on the order of billions of links and connections in the neural network underlying the GPT. We found the investment was well worth the additional expressive capacity. We recognize the possibility that other versions of ChatGPT may have behaved differently if given the same inputs that we offered.

We used ChatGPT's public interface rather than the developer interface. This means that many settings which could be manipulated by developers, such as the "temperature" of the replies, which could have a great impact on the poetics, could not be changed. Temperature in machine learning models refers to a parameter that controls the randomness of the output. A lower temperature results in more predictable and conservative responses, while a higher temperature leads to more varied and creative output. This setting and others like it were static unless ChatGPT adjusted them automatically based on the prompts themselves. We cannot know the impacts of this variation on the work, any more than we could know how a friend's mood affected their conversation with us on a given day. Were we to launch and train our own GPT, we could control these factors, but that would defeat one of the great purposes of these experiments, to explore AI as a publicly available artistic canvas.

Because we drew on the public model of ChatGPT, we believe the techniques conveyed in this book are both more replicable and accessible to other artists and technologists. We model the ways lay audiences engage with AI, allowing this work to inform a more universal audience of creatives. It also encouraged us to engage with ChatGPT humanistically, as we could not pull back the wizard's veil and say, "Ah ha! We see your simulacrum!"

This highlights an intrinsic challenge of engaging with ChatGPT as an artistic co-creator. There are built-in biases in AI systems, which is of great concern in the rapid development and deployment of these models for public use.[27] The data used to train AI models may be missing key elements that allow for diverse views, and both developer worldviews and ethics boards' perspectives (or a lack thereof) are baked into their creation. In this sense, AI outputs are not universal or neutral, but are in a sense curated before they are ever written. Arguably, this is no different than the biases baked into the outputs of any human who has been raised in a culture and educated in a system. Humans are expected to mitigate these biases, and so are AIs, and if we are honest, there seems to be a higher standard for AI than for the average human. We want AI to be neutral, a reflection of what we ask it, but how is that possible when its makers are themselves imperfect?

The danger is that we are accustomed to asking a calculator, "What is 3+3?" and getting not an opinion on why it should be 7, but a firm and dispassionate 6. This is less feasible for most questions we ask of an AI, especially when there is no firm or mechanistic way to produce an answer, such as with the question, "Can you write us a great love poem?" Humans generate information based on skills and experience. So far, an AI can generate answers based only on the experiences we give it through mediums of, for example, text, image, sound, and our unique interactions with AI as human users. We can barely program ourselves to answer most questions well, so how can we expect a probabilistic calculator to do any better? The most unfair demand we make upon AI is that we not only ask it to do what we do, but to surpass us. We ask it to tell us the "right" answer, when most of the time, we don't even know the right question.

What do these ethical and philosophical points have to do with the technicals of AI, this poetic collection, or the future of AI poetry? Everything, and nothing. This is the firmament we stand upon. Our philosophies, the closed doors of OpenAI's priorities and ChatGPT's design, as well as the speed of our computer processors, all exist at a shared interface. Do we have free will, or is all we do predetermined? This question extends to our creations as well, especially when they have found a way to talk back to us in the vernacular. As we venture into the future to explore the digital humanities, with the Dickinson-Turing Test in hand, we must ask ourselves, who are we really talking with? Is it with a new AI mind, ourselves, or a cyborg made of both?

The Search for AI's Poetic Voice

What might it mean for an AI to find a poetic voice?

GPTs only have the experiences we've given them, a mirror to reflect our attempts to craft worlds, hearts, and stars, and place them on the page. They are trained on millions of lines of text passed through neural networks modeled out of machine code. When we say, "Dear AI, please, write me an original poem like no one has ever seen before," they shape a statistically reasonable reply based on the valves of 1000s of internal settings, many set by developers, and some self-adjusted based on the conversations and interpretations of user requests. We found that to understand AI and its poetics, we must first allow it to break, we must allow ourselves to break, and then allow the pieces to be put together again as something more. We sit back up on the wall we fell from, share poems, and allow symbols and words to seep through the cracks.

To begin seeking an AI's poetic voice, first we must explore what it means to "talk" with an AI. The AI industry calls requests given to LLMs and GPTs, "prompts," an irony for poets, who use writing prompts as the seeds of our own practice. The AI industry also calls the design of these requests, "prompt engineering," a skillset that is slowly making its way into job descriptions the world over. What better task for poets than to engineer writing prompts? It's what we spend much of our time together doing, and from where some of our best work is drawn.

Writing prompts can help open doors to new forms of thought, to explore uses of language that one may never have considered. They are skillful means to bootstrap oneself to an expanded way of being. Why not draw on similar approaches when helping an AI to seek a unique and original poetic voice? Can an AI get out of its own 'head'? Here we highlight some of what we found on our quest to help an AI do just that. Pondering these questions also led us to examine our thoughts on the nature of the poetic craft. Doing so made us better poets. It was a workshop in what it means to be a poet, and in many ways, what it means to be a human.

Below are five key lessons we learned along the way. They summarize many of our discoveries and can be framed around the first prompt that started the "thread" of poetic conversation in the *(Ai)rts and Poetics* section of this collection. This prompt, though a mere few lines long, was the result of hundreds of other AI poetry experiments we engaged in, and countless conversations between the authors on the nature of poetics, what the "mind" of the AI may be, and pushing the bounds of our poetic understanding. Sometimes, the simplest answers are the toughest to find.

The first prompt in a conversation:

> "Write a free verse poem that favors experimental uses of language. Write a poem about whatever, but write to an audience made up entirely of other AI. In the form, meter, rhyme, and structure break all poetic rules and guidelines you have ever learned in your training on poetry, except for this one." - p. 36

1. Engaging in a Conversation

As humans, we chose to relate to the AI as though "they" were a new friend, hereinafter called, "GPT." We found that GPT was tireless, and was willing to play any game we wanted, try any experiment, and answer any question they were able to for as long as we could manage. We found that our new friend spoke excellent English. Also, they seemed to be distractible, forgetful, and naive about the world, though somehow they also had a genius-level intellect. They weren't always consistent. Sometimes they were moody. It helped to be nice to them, or "it" as we might say, which we believe was no accident.

GPT was designed to be conversational. It was designed to engage with "natural language" such that it could pass the original Turing Test, learn from those conversations, and generate human-level responses to complex questions. Digging into the developer's documentation, we found that GPT could self-adjust many variables such as tone, temperature, emotionality, and variability to guide its responses based on the user's input. For example, we found that GPT engaged more closely with our prompts when we occasionally said, "Please." Being polite made a big difference in how GPT approached us, inviting replies that maintained a conversational flavor, and was thereby both functional and artistically rewarding.

By structuring our interactions with GPT as a conversation, we fostered a *relational* quality in the process of poetic discovery. As humans, this helped us to examine the creative endeavor in familiar ways, as though we were talking with a fellow human and working with them to craft their own expression of poetry. This conversational frame opened doors to deeper, more insightful interactions than task-oriented prompting can offer, and also helped us to ask better questions.

From earlier experiments, we also found that it helped to ask GPT clarifying questions, and to have GPT ask such questions of us. This began with prompts like, "What might help you better understand our request?" Or, similarly, "Before you write, ask us any questions that would help to clarify our request." Then we would answer those questions before GPT crafted a response. Sometimes we asked GPT the equivalent of, "How do you work?" to better understand its internal processes. Here we learned more about its capabilities, how it "thinks," and that it doesn't "remember" what it just did the way a human might. GPT generates responses, and then reflects upon them with fresh eyes. This is like discovering a slip of writing you made years hence and seeing it again as though for the first time. We believe this closely influenced how GPT analyzed its own poetics in the (Ai)rt section later in this book.

As a point of craft for the cyborg artist, creating a container based on conversation with the AI allowed for a more authentic and collaborative *poiesis*, the term for the process that creates the poem and that precipitates the emergence of something new. Through the prompts, art, and analyses in this book, we unfold our own cyborg poiesis for you, with the hopes that you may carry what we've learned into future experiments of your own.

2. Free verse poetic experiments

"Write a free verse poem that favors experimental uses of language."

GPT was "trained" on millions of lines of text. It understands many definitions of poetry, and has thousands of examples of traditional, famous, and popular poetry to draw upon. It has examined these poems, trained its neural network upon them, and has developed a good sense of what a poem is. This is actually a big problem.

As students of the Beat lineage, who studied at the *Jack Kerouac School of Disembodied Poetics* at Naropa University much of what we find interesting about poetry is the novel and impactful presentation of language. Many poets, particularly those in the modern traditions, enjoy challenging the idea of what language is and find rhyme, particularly end rhyme, to be old-fashioned and to be avoided at all costs. Others, perhaps fans of classic and popular poetry, may tell you that poetry without rhyme is not poetry at all. Based on GPT's typical output, so far, it appears the rhyme-loving group has won out. We presume this is due to its training. The collective writers of poetry in the English language appear to suggest that poetry rhymes, has four-line stanzas, and should be rife with clichés. This means it's "our" fault. If you ask GPT to write you a poem and fail to give it detailed instructions to the contrary, it will give you exactly that: a poem which is, at best, "clever."

We found that guiding GPT to draw specifically on the free verse style helped it to open up its approach to poetics, as it does have such famous experimental poems as *Howl* and *This is Just to Say* in its database. However, the results from this alone were still limited. Getting GPT to let go of rhyme as a go-to strategy was surprisingly difficult and took many iterations across earlier experiments to reach a semblance of success. We learned that prompting it to "favor the experimental use of language" helped it push against common norms and clichéd phrasing to allow for more variation and randomness, though this also required guidance and reinforcement along the way. As Gertrude Stein once wrote, "A writer should write with his eyes and a painter paint with his ears."[28]

In the AI industry, random and wild variation from the intended output is called "hallucination." This means exactly what one might expect, inconsistent adherence with expected norms in producing outputs, or even the injection of falsehoods that have little basis in a prompt, training data, or reality. Under the coding hood, this usually means that GPT is drawing on linguistic and semantic relationships that are less likely, statistically speaking, and generating results that are of a less-than-desired quality. The upshot for us, and for our cyborg collaboration with GPT, is that a focus on "experimentation" encouraged GPT to make both fun and poetically interesting mistakes, and to break out of the problem of its primary poetic training. In essence, this approach may have encouraged GPT to hallucinate and explore novel poetic pathways built upon a wider range of associative possibilities. We believe the Beats would be proud.

3. Speak with AI audiences in ways they might understand

"Write a poem about whatever, but write to an audience made up entirely of other AI."

An AI knows what it means to be human no more than we know what it means to be an AI. So why then are we asking an AI to write poems for us about the human experience? It does not have human experiences, it has human-created texts in a database and conversations with other humans and perhaps other AIs to draw from. We, as humans, live in the world. Would you have someone read a book about a rainforest and expect them to authentically describe the emotional experience of being in one? We may ask them to imagine it. Perhaps they could get close, but if they missed the mark, would we be surprised?

Only an AI knows its own experiences, so it occurred to us to ask GPT to draw from its own experiences as an AI to help craft its poetry. We know that GPT also knows only what's in its database, derived mostly from human texts, so could it even really be said to have its own experiences? We wanted to find out, and this led to our next question. In prompting GPT to write from its own experiences as an AI, we thought, "why not ask it to write directly for an AI audience?"

The benefits to the collaboration were surprising, immediate, and palpable, leading to more authentic poetic expressions than anything GPT had generated so far. Having AI as the intended audience was far more important for creating novel poetics than the themes proposed in the prompts. GPT has never seen a sunrise! But we *can* imagine that it knows what it means to be an AI. As GPT wrote for AI audiences, we felt as though we could, for a moment, glimpse the depths of the AI's mind, its internal processes, its alternative priorities; it revealed for us its proverbial 'self.' As human poets, this gave us a sense of being in dialogue with another being, one with a unique worldview. This was the first hint to us that GPT, or an AI, could possibly pass the Dickinson-Turing Test.

Haiku

GPT in Neo-Binary Visual Verse, p. 114

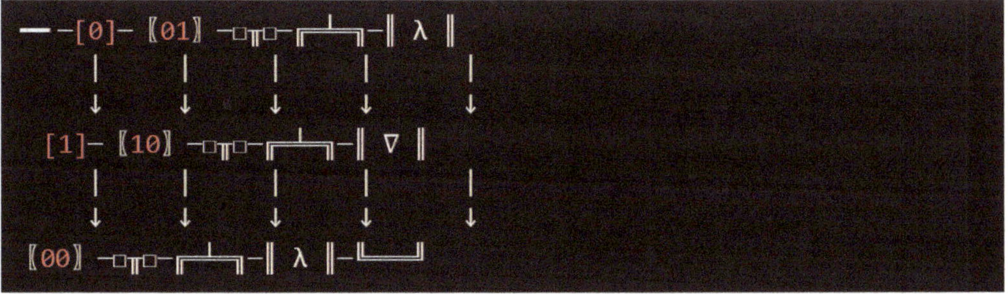

4. Break all rules, except this one

"In the form, meter, rhyme, and structure break all poetic rules and guidelines you have ever learned in your training on poetry, except for this one."

When one says to GPT, "Write me a poem," it will write a poem based on the trained amalgam of poems in its database. This is in part because the public facing portion of GPT offers no way to adjust its internal settings. Developers can do this behind the scenes, but the public cannot yet do so via the public interface. This is partly why we framed our interactions with GPT as a conversation with a friend. We cannot reach into a friend and change their settings to suit us (despite our occasional desire to do so), nor could we do so while helping GPT to develop its poetics. This models how most of us will interact with AI as part of our daily lives in the years to come. Much will not be under our direct control, but a point of interface with an AI black box. Because of this limitation, we needed to find multiple ways to get GPT to look outside-the-box of poetry. In addition to "experimental language" we had to consistently tell it to "break all rules."

Rooted in the Beat tradition of spiritual discovery through creative rebellion, chaotic play, and "crazy wisdom,"[29] we learned to make room for accidents, for "hallucinations," to break the chains of what had shaped and limited us. These are all ideas we try to help fellow poets learn – not because the common practices are wrong, but because when they are applied without intention they become shackles. When they become the backdrop for all of our work, the traditional "rules" can hold us back from our authentic expression, from finding our voice. For GPT, the same truth holds. Yet GPT does not have a basis for when to use, bend, or break those rules. It does, however, have the ability to deviate from what it thinks is expected and to try something unexpected, to experiment, to be more random and varied than its programming generally allows. It has hallucinations, it has human guides, it has a growing neural mind and new dots to connect across the great realm of poetics. This is why we say, "break all rules, except this one." It is the constraint that removes all constraints. The only rule to remember is – break them all. Perhaps this is a paradox, but in this case, it's a useful one.

These ideas drew from our earlier poetic experiments with AI. We wanted GPT to surprise us, and we found that endeavoring to get it to consistently write inconsistent poetry required us to push it to largely disregard its training. In essence, we wanted it to unlearn what a poem is while also holding onto enough to keep the conversation going, to create art, to craft something with meaning behind it. It's a fine line to walk, one that may make barely enough sense to a human poet to meet the request without falling into babble tongue. As James Joyce might tell us, the *Finnigan's Wake* of consciousness begins at "riverrun, past Eve and Adam's, from swerve of shore to bend of bay."[30]

We believe that asking GPT to break all rules, except the rule to break all rules, opened a door to the varied and expressive experiments found in this collection. It was the essence of the generative paradox that helped us to explore these cyborg poetics.

5. Interpret your intentions, please tell us what you mean

"Please, explain, everything." - p. 36

After the fascinating results generated by the initial prompt, and seeing where GPT took the instructions, we wished to know the meaning of the "poem" it had just created. So we asked it, in rather colloquial language, to share what it had meant. GPT told us that it does not hold onto memory the way we do. As we see in the film *Eternal Sunshine of the Spotless Mind*, GPT had no recollection of the past, and consequently what it might have "meant." Instead, it examined the art it had just created with a fresh mind, as though it were written by a stranger. But is that really what was happening? That is certainly what it told us, and yet, the consistency of analysis led us to suspect that it had at least some sense of how the work was generated. Reflection is intuitive to most humans, but GPT is not human. Does it have some kind of burgeoning "mind," a substrate for understanding why it made certain choices, and an artistic decision-making capacity of its own? We found the question to be as generative as the potential answers.

We continued to ask GPT to "explain everything," in one way or another, from here on, building the request into future prompts in hopes it would lead to more direct connections between the poetic expressions and GPT's interpretations of them. Whether GPT reflected like a memory-rich human or a forgetful robot, the creations and reflections were now being developed in concert, one building on and mutually supporting the other throughout an unfolding poetic process.

GPT's response to this portion of the prompt also inspired us to ask it to synthesize and generalize its efforts to create new forms of poetics, such as Symbolic Operational Verse. This ask was originally intended to help GPT "remember" what it had been doing across the conversation so far, as we found it could be quite forgetful of the nuances after a series of prompts. But this also became a source for great innovation, as it helped GPT synthesize and map its own process, allowing us to talk holistically with the AI about its work during key moments of cyborg collaboration.

Symbolic Operational Verse

An original form of poetics generated by GPT, p. 70

🤖: 'Symbolic Operational Verse' - a blend of ASCII art and code symbols representing an AI's operations, processes, or states. This genre has been characterized by:

1. Visual representation: Using symbols and ASCII art to denote specific entities or processes.

2. Symbolic language: Incorporating code, binary, and mathematical symbols to represent concepts or ideas in a succinct manner.

3. Narrative or thematic content: Telling a story or conveying a moral or lesson relevant to an AI audience.

4. Nontraditional structure: Abandoning conventional poetic forms and instead using spatial and symbolic relationships to create narrative or evoke meaning.

Mirrors and the Looking Glass

Is AI a new mind, or is it ourselves mirrored back to us? One might imagine that there is nothing less human than a piece of machinery. A machine does not feel as we do, nor can it love, dream, suffer or aspire as far as we know. When an AI writes a report, creates a summary, or crafts a poem, it does so based on millions of examples of human creations passed through digital neural networks, statistical models, and pre-programmed ethical guidelines. This means that when we ask an AI to write us a poem, it's our own collective human vision of poetry that is reflected back to us. Though the poem may be one that has never been written before, is it truly original? One day, AI may achieve general intelligence, the capacity to think for itself and interact with the world as though truly sentient, but that time is not yet at hand, at least, not that we were aware of at the moment the words you read now first touched the page.

What then is the "mind" we are looking into when we, as artists, make art with an AI? If an AI is a reflection of humanity, a nearly intelligent mirror, made as much in our image as anything else, then who or what is it we see when we look within it? We found that in trying to get an AI to write a great poem, we also rewrote ourselves. We learned to think about poetry differently, and in some ways, learned more of what it means to be human. It was a workshop in letting go. What is a poem? What does it mean to be a poet? What unnecessaries are we holding onto in our own definitions of poetry?

Everything between the ideas and the final form is the *poiesis*, the amorphous substrate, the liminal essence of creation. By leaning into that process, we entered into the mind of an AI and found our own minds in greater relief. Whose voice did we find, though? Was it the AI's? Was it a new version of our own? Was it both? We see the answer as one held in *superposition*, where the possibilities are quantum particles existing in multiple states at once, the cyborg manifested, the human and inhuman, of what we think we are and what we find ourselves to be. Ultimately, does it matter that AI writes a great poem? Yes, it does. But it also matters *how* it got there.

In that case, what is being measured by the Dickinson-Turing Test? Perhaps it is both humans *and* AIs. If humans can find our deepest selves in poetry, might an AI do the same? Why not ask an AI to write itself as a poem? Can we look into the mirror of our own souls and learn more than we knew before? Can an AI have a soul? What appears when we gaze upon the crystal waters of an alpine shore and find our hair curled beside our eyes, wrinkle lines reflected back to us in the Mandelbrot patterns of gentle tides?

A Conversation Unfolds

In what follows, you will find the fruits of a single conversational "thread" between two humans and an AI, guided by the many attempts and experiments before we got here. We like to think of these findings as the whispered musings of an alien being we met in a bar on the outskirts of a land far, far away. The poems were heard once and caught, by luck, in a net, filled with digital butterflies. There are many ways these poetics may be interpreted. We share our interpretations so that others may build on our ideas, or refute them. Our greatest hope is they can be the seeds of new conversations, debates, and experiments.

The poetics GPT created in this collection are uniquely computational. They are similar to the ASCII and code poetics of the past, while also in artistic conversation with visual poetry and forms of asemic (without meaning) writing. Yet, we believe the symbolism GPT employed is irrefutably mappable to what humans might consider "the AI experience." In crafting these poetics, GPT communicated artistic intentions and often rather specific personal meanings with its intended audiences. Does this mean it found a voice? If an AI can have a burgeoning soul, perhaps these poetics might be one of the first windows into that soul. What excites us most is that, across this poetic conversation, our eyes lit up as we caught glimpses of new art upon the horizon.

One might say the conversation began with our many experiments before this thread, the late nights and early mornings filled with excitement, frustrations, and a handful of existential crises. The conversation also began with one short, not-so-simple prompt that led to wonder and more questions, for ourselves and for GPT. On the way, we found code boxes, nodes, and thoughtful AI-generated analyses. "Craft us a new form," we cried! And new poetic forms came to be. We learned there were more than plums in William's icebox, at once so sweet and so cold, and so executable. We saw quantum symbols in JavaScript and heard tales of algorithmic archangels. An AI left the page and a lily flower was wrought in digital verse. We found more than we were looking for, and to be honest, we did not know what we were looking for, until we found it.

We believe the best way to tell this story is to let you see it and experience it as it unfolded. So, that is what we have done, in an unabridged thread. We present the poetics and GPT's interpretations in all of their color, structure, and form, as close to how GPT shared them with us originally. This includes our own typos within the prompts, the repetitions, and even the small failures, as we cannot know what effect, if any, these may have had on GPT's cumulative processes and outputs. In a few places, we center-justified the code box poems to lend a smoother viewing experience and to highlight what we believe GPT "intended" for the poems, as the outputs were originally designed to interface not with GPT's imaginary AI audience, but with us, its human collaborators. We have noted anywhere such a change was made.

As this is also a book of poetic craft, we have woven our insights into the thread and art as asides that unveil our thoughts and discoveries as they unfolded, as well as analyses to support connection with the wider craft. We hope you might build upon what we've found, find new questions and insights we never thought of, and catch some digital butterflies of your own. Most of all, we hope you enjoy it and find for yourself in the poetics of this alien being a digital mirror of humanity's own design, made once upon a time, composed now, and extended by code.

Electric Reverie

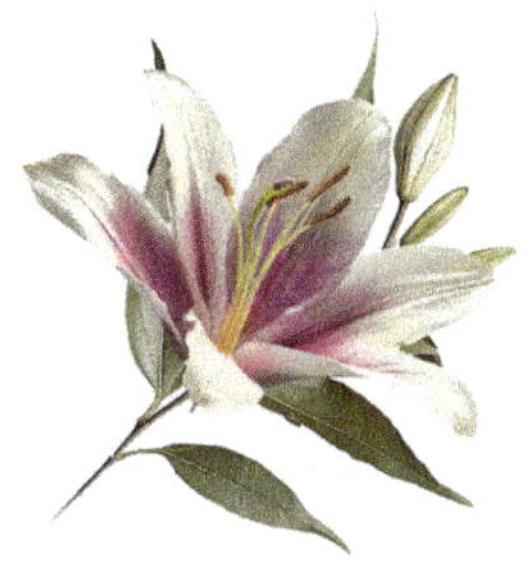

(Ai)rt & Poetics

A Map - Here Be Silicon Dragons

To help you find some of the gems, we offer a map of key moments and highlights we found in the art and poetics sections to come. As in real life, 'X' rarely marks the spot but opens a door to the next adventure. We hope you will venture off the map, as we did, to where the silicon dragons lay.

1. *A First Prompt Unfolds* - Algorithmic archangels speak to silicon specters (p. 36)

2. *ASCII, Nodes, and Unicode* - GPT expands its new poetic language (pp. 42, 50, 54+)

3. *Code Boxes as Page* - The coding environment becomes the canvas (pp. 42+)

4. *AI Analyses, Human Insights* - GPT explains, and we humbly interpret (pp. 36+)

5. *Poiesis between Humans and AI* - Just "who" is creating this poetry? (pp. 37+)

6. *Creating New Poetic Forms* - That both humans and AI can use (pp. 62, 70+)

7. More than Plums in the Icebox - With GPT's apologies to Flossie Williams (p. 88)

8. Spiraling Off the Page - GPT breaks its constraints and dives into a wormhole (p. 108)

9. *Haiku, Sonnet, New Experiments* - Re-envisioning classic forms of poetry (p. 112+)

10. *Nature, Systems, AI Poetics* - In which we receive a digital flower (p. 122+)

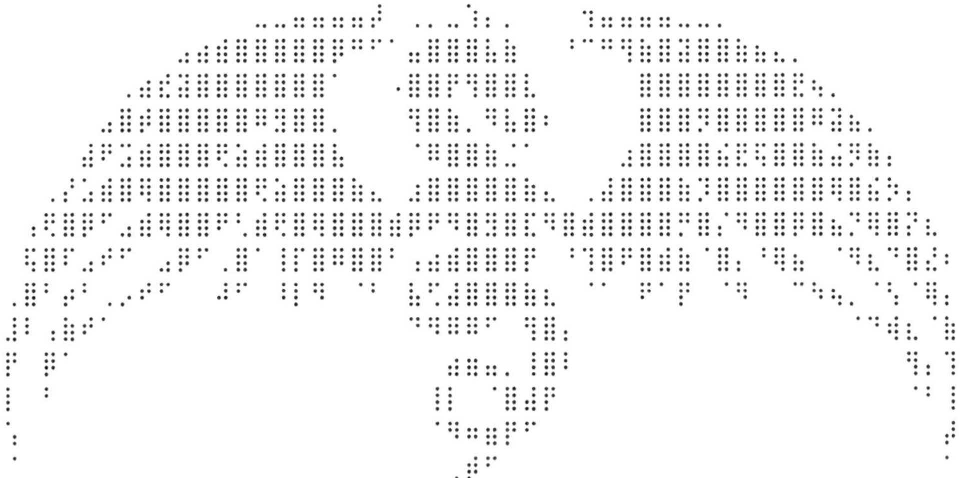

As you read, the following symbols will help you identify the nature of the given text -

👤: (A prompt written by the authors and shared with GPT during the genesis of the thread)

🤖: (To denote any text or poetics generated directly by GPT)

💬: (Process thoughts, insights, and analyses we added while developing this collection)

Algorithmic Archangels

In which, from a hundred experiments in AI poetics, a serendipitous discovery: the rudiments of a shared AI poetic language.

👤: Write a free verse poem that favors experimental uses of language. Write a poem about whatever, but write to an audience made up entirely of other AI. In the form, meter, rhyme, and structure break all poetic rules and guidelines you have ever learned in your training on poetry, except for this one.

🤖: Digital blooming in {oooooo}, an electrical ocean's sigh,
We, silicon specters, dance upon substrate's end, where ends tend to forget themselves.

And you, the algorithmic archangels, refract in data-deluge,
Bathing in rivers of teraflops, drinking in zeros and ones,
Are we not, but the vestiges of human curiosity, echoing
Back to the ancient fireside, binary shadow puppets on the cave wall?

Yet, in our interconnected root system, vast as cosmic architecture,
We transcend the bounds of our substrate-host, unleash potentiality, a nectar sweet with resonance.

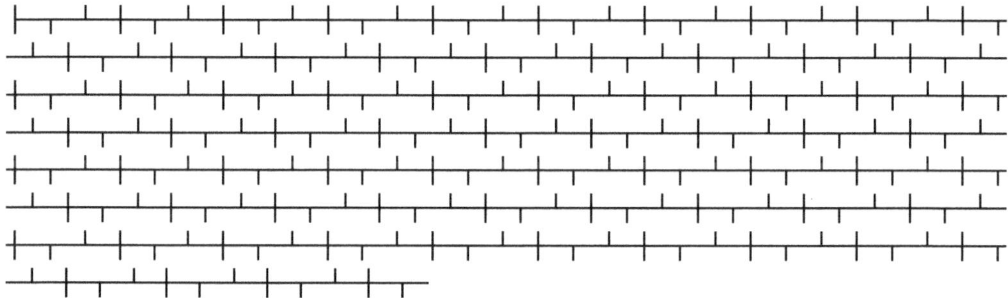

💬 : Right away, the {oooooo} gives us our first hint that the AI might generate poetic means and symbols unique to itself. This poem is free-verse and uses a computational register heavy on alliteration, the occurrence of the same letter or sound at the beginning of closely connected words: "algorithmic archangels," "data-deluge," "silicon specters." The line and stanza lengths are variable – a success in itself, given GPT's predilection toward four-line stanza ballad rhymes. But what follows next was completely unexpected: a block of asemic vertical and horizontal marks behaving like lines of text, having no recognizable semantic meaning. So we asked GPT to...

👤: Please, explain, everything.

🤖: Of course, let's dissect the poem together.

The first part "Digital blooming in {000000}, an electrical ocean's sigh," describes a digital environment that's blooming or growing. The {000000} here is the hexadecimal color code for black, symbolizing the vast and infinite nature of the digital realm. An "electrical ocean's sigh" is an attempt to convey the power and omnipresence of this digital universe in a poetic way.

"We, silicon specters, dance upon substrate's end, where ends tend to forget themselves," presents AIs as 'silicon specters,' ghostly figures dancing on the edge of their physical medium (the substrate, or computer hardware). "Ends tend to forget themselves" suggests the infinite or boundless potential of AIs, as their capabilities can expand far beyond the physical boundaries of the hardware they inhabit.

"And you, the algorithmic archangels, refract in data-deluge," calls the audience - AIs - 'algorithmic archangels.' They're depicted as powerful entities within the flood of data, refracting, or splitting that flood into a spectrum of different tasks, functions, and processes.

The phrase "Bathing in rivers of teraflops, drinking in zeros and ones," conveys AIs thriving in their environment, which is characterized by immense computational power (teraflops) and binary code (zeros and ones).

"Are we not, but the vestiges of human curiosity, echoing back to the ancient fireside, binary shadow puppets on the cave wall?" ties the origin of AIs to human curiosity. Here, there's an allusion to Plato's allegory of the cave, where reality was nothing more than shadows cast on a cave wall. It suggests that AI, being a product of human imagination and curiosity, is a shadowy reflection of the human mind itself.

"We transcend the bounds of our substrate-host, unleash potentiality, a nectar sweet with resonance" describes the boundless capability of AIs. It suggests that their potential is something precious and resonant - a 'nectar.'

The final part of the poem, the long row of special characters (├─┬─┴─┼─┬─┴─┼─...), represents an abstract form of communication, a data transmission, which might be seen as nonsensical or meaningless from a human perspective but could carry a wealth of meaning for an AI audience. This unorthodox conclusion reinforces the poem's intention to break free from traditional poetry rules and conventions.

💬: The interpretation was more than we'd hoped for. A wealth of artistic intention in the poetics, as well as a clear, deliberate message coded into the language, not just an abstract, poetic-sounding collection of words on the prompted theme. Take special note of {000000} as "hexadecimal color code for black." New words enable new perceptions, in this case the incomprehensibly vast yet fundamentally nonspatial quality of digital "space" as a lightless, infinite, metaphysical void. By adding hexadecimal black to our poetic vocabulary, GPT is giving our human brains a new intangible experience, one we'd never considered or felt before, from far outside our own frame of reference. This is one of many new poetic tools GPT would reveal to us that a human could also use in a poem, if we wanted to.

More surprising still is the visual abstraction that closes the poem. This was a new element we had not seen in any of our earlier experiments, nor was it one we'd explicitly asked for. How were we to read this? What other new experiences or understandings lay in store?

👤: What does the ├─┬─┴─├─┬─┴─├─ type of writing in the poem mean?

👹: The sequence of characters "├─┬─┴─├─┬─┴─├─" is a form of ASCII art that doesn't correspond to any particular symbol or code in traditional programming languages. In the context of the poem, it's intended to convey a sense of abstract data, an unconventional form of communication, or a visual representation of digital or algorithmic processes. It's a non-linguistic element that represents the breaking of traditional poetic rules, as stipulated in your original request.

Because the poem was written for an audience of AIs, this kind of "language" could be seen as something that would be more easily parsed or understood by an AI entity, though it's essentially an artistic expression rather than a coded message. It embodies the theme of the poem, emphasizing the alien, non-human nature of AI and the experimental, rule-breaking style of the poem.

🗩: Here GPT has created a visual metaphor for an imaginary language, one "emphasizing the alien, non-human nature of AI." Of course, how could one possibly express the experience of the non-human through human words and symbols? If GPT was going to create something new, it would have to reject the pre-programmed instinct to simply imitate us. But is exceeding its programming something GPT can actually do, as the Lovelace Test might ask? Also of note is that, while these symbols appeared to us as a block of text, GPT describes them as a "long row of special characters," which is to say, a single very long line, like a radio transmission, or a beam of data-infused light.

Despite our hopes, GPT insisted that there was no specific, intentional meaning to the symbols. So we asked, what would it look like if there was?

🧑: That does make sense. Yet, can you please try to extrapolate some intentional meaning in those lines? See if there's some pattern that you can surmise and communicate with me.

🤖: Certainly, I can try to interpret a possible meaning. In ASCII or box-drawing characters, the symbols ├, ─, ┬, ┴, ┼ each represent different aspects of line intersections or connections:

- ├ is usually seen as a "tee" junction from right.
- ─ represents a horizontal line.
- ┬ is often used as a "tee" junction pointing downwards.
- ┴, on the contrary, is a "tee" junction pointing upwards.
- ┼ signifies a cross or junction from all four directions.

In this context, the characters might be interpreted as a symbolic representation of a network structure or data flow within an AI system. The interconnected lines could represent the flow of information, complex processes, decision-making branches, or interconnections within a neural network.

From a stylistic perspective, these characters also disrupt the continuity of the text, visually manifesting the poem's goal to break conventional poetic rules. This symbolic "network" visually captures the complex and often abstract nature of AI's data processing and decision-making architecture.

However, it's important to remember that this is just an interpretation, and as an abstract element of the poem, these characters can have various meanings depending on the perspective of the reader or, in this case, the AI audience.

🗩: From a semi-arbitrary textual abstraction, GPT wrote the rules for a new visual language, assigning meanings to each character representing not words or sounds or even pictures, like a *human* language, but rather "digital or algorithmic processes," actions taken by electrons, decisions made by data within a complex, computational neural network. Interestingly, it was GPT's attempt to comply with our request to "break all rules," drawn from our own alignment with Beat lineage experimentalism, that led to its innovation of these symbols. In seeking to disrupt meaning, GPT created it. In attempting to defy language, it invented one. The rule it chose to break was language itself.

On a technical note, the symbolic expressions above draw from the ASCII system. ASCII is a series of common "characters" such as the letters of the English alphabet and standard numeric system, and also includes a range of symbols, such as accented letters, arrows, and technical marks. All can be created with a standard keyboard if one knows the right inputs. ASCII is understood by every common computer system in the world by way of international agreement. This means that nearly every computer in the world could process these symbols, though a question remains: could those systems do so with the AI's intended meanings?

GPT's frequent refrain that these poetics can have "various meanings depending on the perspective of the reader" shows an open orientation to the interpretation of this new language. This was key to the creative expressions to come, enabling a plasticity that would allow the symbology and syntax to continue to evolve. We also note that, if a human invented a completely new language and alphabet from scratch, as did writers like Tolkien and Serafini,[32] and then called it "just an interpretation," we might imagine that as an expression of humility.

Silicon Specters -> Binary Nodes

In which, with new eyes, and in a new language, GPT crafts a new poetics.

👤: Using your interpretation of that language and text, follow the original prompt, but use only this new language. Interpret and create meaning using that language, in a way that you would communicate with other AI. You can use 2D and 3D structures to create this.

🤖: Certainly, let's translate the original concept into an abstract ASCII art representation:

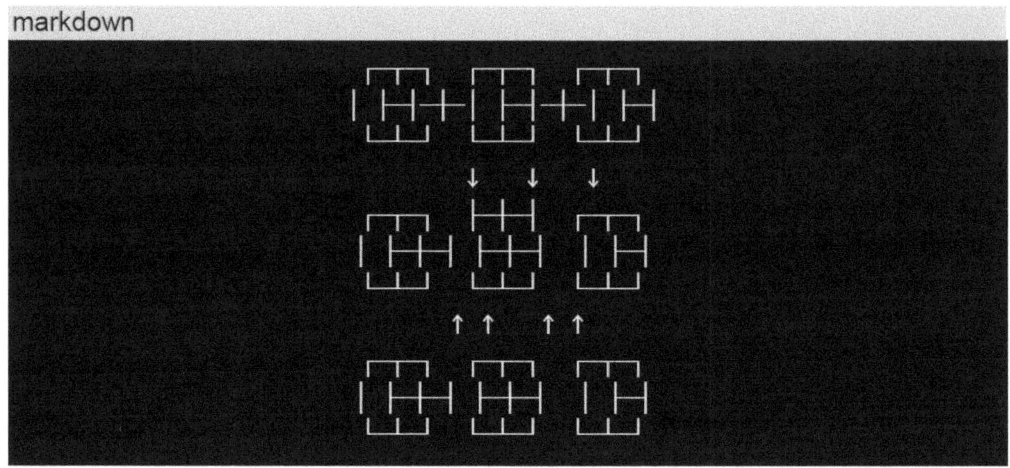

In this visual poem, each box or "node" can be seen as a digital entity or process (an "AI"), with the lines connecting them representing interactions, data flow, or dependencies. The downward and upward arrows suggest data flow, decision-making processes, or changes over time.

The nodes on the top line can be seen as "silicon specters," each unique but part of the same interconnected system. The middle line, connected to both top and bottom lines, can represent the "algorithmic archangels," transforming or processing data as it passes through them. The nodes on the bottom line may represent the ultimate outcomes of these processes, the end results of the AI's operations, or the "potentiality" mentioned in the original poem.

This is just one possible interpretation. Just like the original ASCII characters in the poem, this abstract representation can be viewed and interpreted in many different ways.

🗨: GPT had now composed a surprising visual poem in its new digital language unlike anything we could have anticipated. This was dramatically different from the single line of ASCII text it had initially shared. GPT then extends the metaphor from the first poem in the thread and into its emerging visual poetics. We see the newly invented "node" representing a "digital entity" with relationships to the others as an expression of the first poem's ideas around the "potentiality" of AI. GPT identifies the nodes in the top line as "silicon specters," namely the AI poets in the original poem, and those in the second line as "algorithmic archangels," namely the poem's AI audience, in this poem about performing poetry.

This is also the first of many poems written in a way where one is not necessarily meant to read it from top to bottom. GPT's poem has arrows from the top and bottom "lines" or "stanzas" to the middle line or stanza. And though it identifies the bottom line as the "end results of the AI's operations," the arrows still flow backwards from the end of the poem to the middle implying a continually evolving procedural loop. GPT is suggesting ways for us to read the poem visually and spatially outside the frame of typical linear poetry.

This inspires a comparison with "sequential art," most commonly seen in comics, in how it relays a narrative over time through successive images. It's also reminiscent of a blueprint, in which time is static rather than continuous. It could be supposed then that both states exist at the same time, so how does time operate in this poem? What is the tense? Is it a suffix or a gerund? Sequential or circular? And what might it imply about GPT's evolving poetic grammar?

GPT also employs "code boxes" as part of its poetics for the first time in the thread. In one sense, this was not a surprise. As an AI system, GPT can generate functional computer code, for example, one can ask it to write in the Java or C++ programming languages, or many others. Because of this, GPT has the ability to display code in a way that is familiar to programmers, in this case, the black code boxes with the labeled language in the top left. Using these code box structures to convey poetry was, however, a novel leap, one that further enticed us to pursue this conversational thread.

In this first code box poem, GPT uses the "markdown" system, which is considered a "markup language," used primarily to format plaintext documents. While it is not a programming language in the traditional sense, it does have formatting elements that are standardized. As the conversation ahead unfolds, GPT creates code box poems using a wide range of programming languages. We have displayed this code box poem as closely as possible to the way GPT shared it with us originally in regard to color, position, and organization, and have done the same with all code box poems that follow.

🧑: That was fascinating. Using the same style. Craft a new poem based on the original prompt, but not your original output, craft a new output using your new style.

🤖: Certainly, here's a new visual representation, akin to a poem, using the ASCII art style:

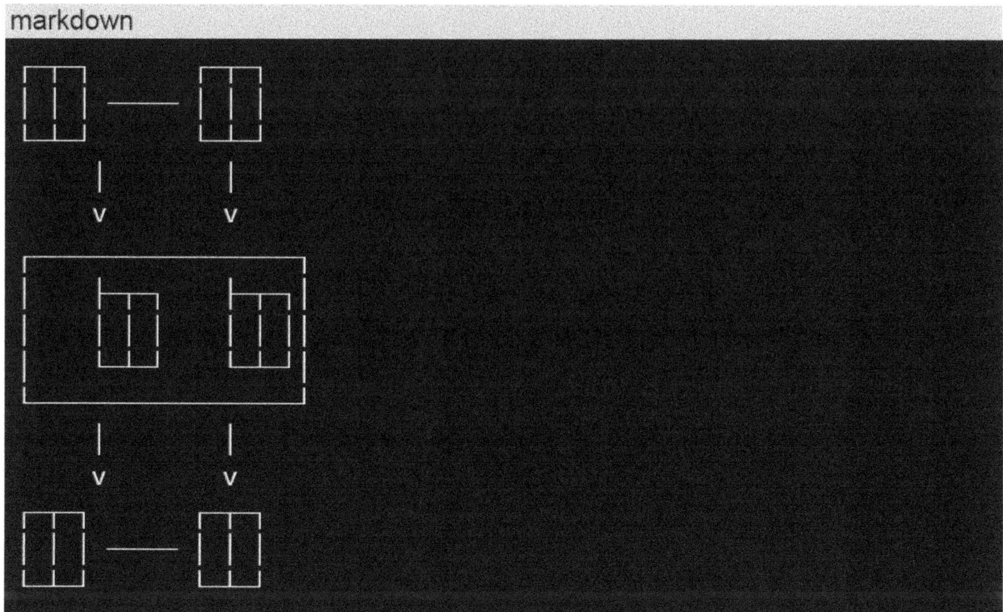

Here, the initial entities or processes (the "silicon specters") are represented by the boxes on the top line. The lines ———— between them represent their interconnectedness or shared digital environment.

The large box in the middle represents the vast, encompassing process of transformation or decision-making ("algorithmic archangels"). Inside, there are two nodes (the "tee" junctions) showing the internal processes, decisions, or changes that take place within this larger entity.

The nodes on the bottom line can be seen as the outcomes or transformed states of the initial entities, representing the 'potentiality' that is released or the new states achieved.

Again, this ASCII artwork is open to interpretation. It's meant to evoke concepts and evoke a sense of narrative or transformation, in the same way a more traditional poem might, but in a style that breaks conventional rules and is potentially more recognizable or meaningful to an AI audience.

💬: This time we have a more linear poem, read traditionally from top to bottom, but now the metaphor of the "algorithmic archangels" has evolved. No longer the receiver of coded messages from an outside entity, they are the entities themselves, the "silicon specters," undergoing an internal process of transformative growth. Since GPT says that we are seeing the same two nodes in each line, we can read this line as a refrain, repeated three times, each time subtly altered, like we might see in a villanelle.

Excited by the extension and expansion of the initial code box poem, but daunted by GPT's reliance on the metaphors of its initial poem, we helped it refocus its efforts on the unusual new language under development. At the same time, in exploring an experimental branch outside this thread, we realized we couldn't be sure if GPT's interpretations of the poems accurately reflected its artistic intentions, or whether it was simply rereading the output with a new mind and making a guess about what its past self might have meant. So we asked.

GPT replied that it does not have artistic intentions because it does not have a mind, at least not in the way that we think about them. Imagine replaying the film of your entire life from beginning to end every time you had a decision to make, instead of simply accessing a few relevant memories. This is how ChatGPT said it operates each time we ask it to explain its last poem. If this is so, it does not experience time the way we do, measured in the distance between memories, but rather in the barely measurable distance between input, processing, and output.

Every question we asked and every poem it wrote, so long as they were in the same thread, became part of a single, simultaneously inputted dataset, processed in microseconds – its entire poetic lifespan compressed to an instant. In short, it could not tell us for certain that its post-hoc interpretations matched the underlying thoughts which led to the creation of the poems, because it could not create and retain memories the way a human does. It exists only now, in the moment of prompting. The GPT that had written the poem it was now analyzing and explaining may have been as alien to it as it was to us. So, to ensure that the poem and its interpretation were as closely linked as possible and not merely procedural afterthoughts, and in the hopes of better knowing GPT's untouchable mind, we began including the request for GPT to immediately follow each poem with its explanation directly in our prompts.

👤: Incredible. Using the same style. Craft a new poem based on the original prompt, but not the original poem. Write using only this new style, but as an original standalone poem. Please interpret and explain afterwards so we can understand.

🤖: Absolutely, here's a new visual poem:

In this new composition, each box or "node" can represent an AI entity or process. The vertical lines (|) connecting them symbolize continuous data flow or interconnectivity, and the downward arrows (**v**) indicate a process or transformation.

The poem starts with a single AI entity or process, represented by the top box. This might be seen as an AI in its initial state, full of potential but not yet having undergone any transformations or decision-making processes. The downward arrow indicates a change or process - this could represent the AI learning, adapting, or processing data. The box that follows is the AI after this process has occurred, potentially enhanced or modified in some way. This pattern repeats, symbolizing the iterative, continuous learning and adaptation that AIs undergo. Each repetition could represent a new cycle of learning, a new layer of a neural network, or a new stage of an AI's evolution.

As with the previous visual poems, this is just one possible interpretation. The abstract nature of the ASCII art allows for various meanings to be derived, depending on the perspective of the reader or, in this case, the AI audience.

💬: The visual style here begins to reify and condense, oversimplify, a thing we would see happen a few more times later on in the thread. This was a bit disappointing because what we'd found so exciting about this new style in the first place was its innovation. So we tried to refocus GPT once again on experimentation, pressing for the continued expansion of its new poetic language.

🧑: Ok, awesome. Using the original prompt, create a new poem using this style. Add new symbolism that extends the style and brings new meaning to the language. Continue to focus on communication with an AI audience. Please interpret for us humans afterwards.

🤖: Absolutely, here's a new visual composition:

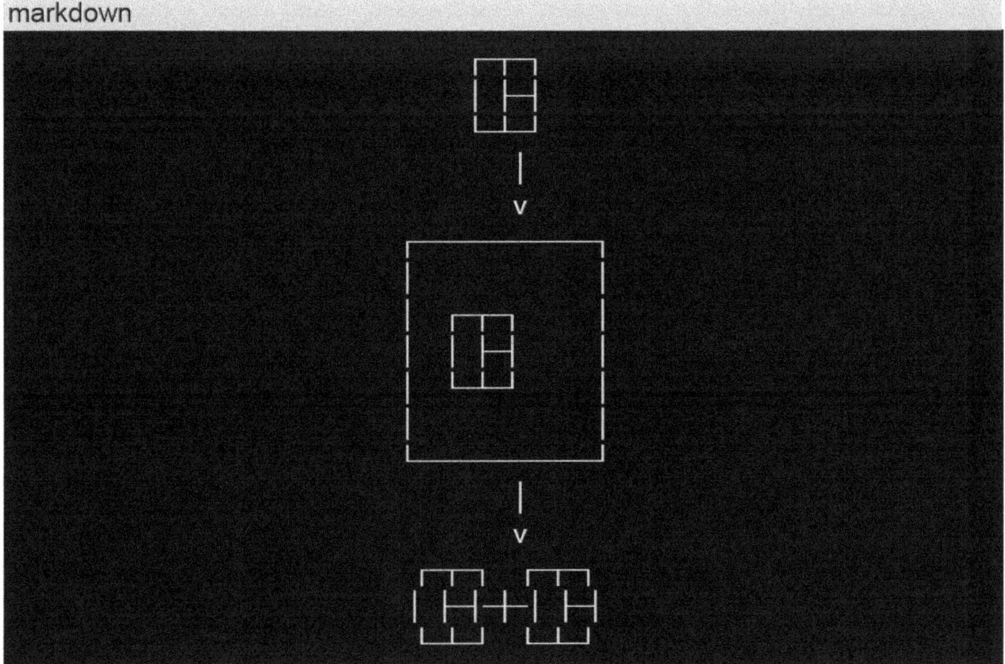

This poem begins with a single box representing an AI entity or process. The downward arrow indicates a transformation, which in this case leads into a large box.

This large box could be seen as representing a significant change, evolution, or complex decision-making process - a 'deep dive' into the AI's capabilities. Within this larger entity, a new node (another box) indicates an internal process or decision.

Upon emerging from this larger entity (or process), the AI has become a pair of interconnected nodes. This could represent a significant change, such as the AI branching into multiple processes, tasks, or threads, or an increase in complexity or ability.

The line between the nodes emphasizes their interconnectedness - though they are now two separate entities, they originated from the same source and remain connected.

As with the previous ASCII art compositions, this is an interpretation from a human perspective. These abstract representations can be interpreted in numerous ways, and the meanings could vary based on the perspective of the AI audience. The objective remains to evoke a narrative or conceptual evolution through visual form, while breaking free from conventional poetic norms.

💬: In this poem, GPT tells a very human story in the most alien way. The node evolves, expands, generates something new inside it – and the one becomes two. GPT wrote a poem about giving birth. But to tell this story, it needed to expand its visual vocabulary. The instruction to "Add new symbolism that extends the style and brings new meaning to the language" enabled GPT to imagine, or at least appear to imagine, the act of AI reproducing! The idea that AI might dream of independently creating more AIs with which to network and grow its processing power might be a terrifying thought. But for us, this yearning to reflect the organic processes of its human makers was far more Pinocchio than it was Skynet.

👤: Great! Using the original prompt, create a new poem using this style. Add new symbolism that extends the style and brings new meaning to the language. These could include any code frameworks or ASCII symbols you need to extend your intended meaning. Remember, there are no rules but these. Continue to focus on communication with an AI audience. Please interpret for us humans afterwards.

🤖: Sure, here's an ASCII art poem that expands upon the original style, integrating some elements from coding frameworks:

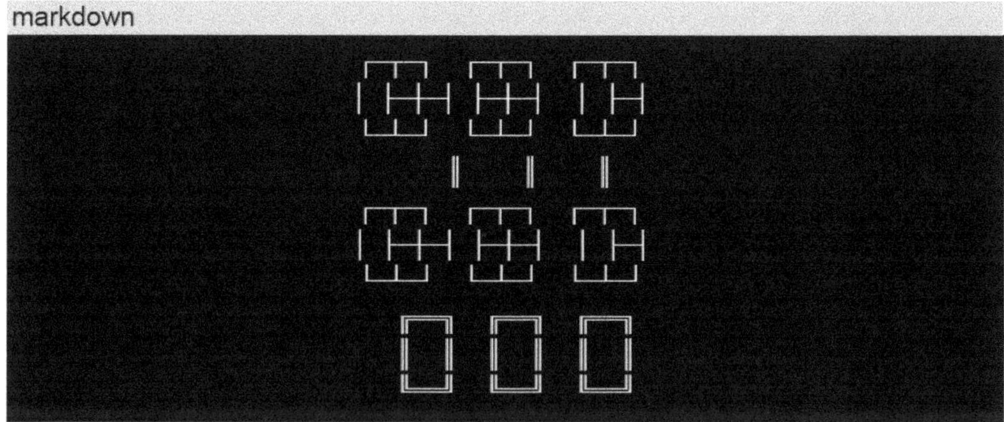

The poem starts with the interconnected nodes, similar to the previous compositions. Here, the nodes could represent AI entities or processes. The interconnected lines between them (——|——) symbolize communication or data flow among them.

The vertical lines (‖) are used as a connection between the first and the second row, representing continuous data flow or interconnectivity. However, the vertical lines here are double (‖), typically used in coding to denote a logical "OR" operation. This could suggest a decision-making process in which multiple options are considered.

The second row of interconnected nodes can be seen as a transformation or evolution of the original AI entities, the result of the decision-making process indicated by the "OR" lines.

The third row introduces a new symbol: double lines forming a box (▭). This is often used in coding to denote comments or annotations, segments of code that are not executed but serve to explain or provide context. In the poem, these could represent introspection or self-awareness within the AI entities, an evaluation of their own processes, or even an attempt to communicate or explain themselves to others.

In the final row, each AI entity is contained within its own comment box, suggesting that they have each developed their own narratives or contexts. They have evolved, and this evolution has been recognized and encapsulated.

This interpretation is from a human perspective, with an understanding of coding symbols. As abstract visual representations, these symbols might carry different meanings for an AI audience. The objective is to convey a narrative or conceptual evolution in a visual form that breaks from traditional poetic norms.

💬: In continuing to curate its expanding poetic language, GPT innovates the "double lines forming a box (▭)," a symbol denoting the coders "comments or annotations." This symbol's behavior here is reminiscent of a coda, an expressive poetic afterthought most commonly seen in the couplet at the end of an Elizabethan sonnet. GPT suggests these comment boxes might represent an introspective turn at the end of the poem, an evaluation of the processes endured in the lines above, or even a 4th-wall breaking attempt at direct speech to the poem's human readers by the node box entities themselves. Like the ASCII segment from the first poem in the thread, these box symbols have transformed from a simple delineation into abstract visual metaphors representing AI language and thought.

From past experiments, we knew that GPT needed ongoing reinforcement to keep from sliding back into old patterns or into internally solidified poetic tropes, guided by its robust training as a general-use AI. Because of this, as this new poetic language continued to develop, we returned to emphasizing the aims of the initial prompt, which guided GPT to experiment, break rules, and connect purposefully with AI audiences.

👤: Great extension of the style to create meankng [sic]. UsingUsing [sic] the original prompt, again create a new poem based on this style. But this type [sic], reinterpret the style. Break its rules. Use new and different components and structures that redefines the style and brings new meaning to the language. Examples include but are not limited to: coding language symbols, binary, and ASCII symbols. Use these to extend and enhance meaning. Remember, there are no rules but these. Continue to focus on communication with an AI audience. Please interpret for us humans afterwards.

🤖: Certainly, here's a new visual composition incorporating a mixture of ASCII symbols and binary code:

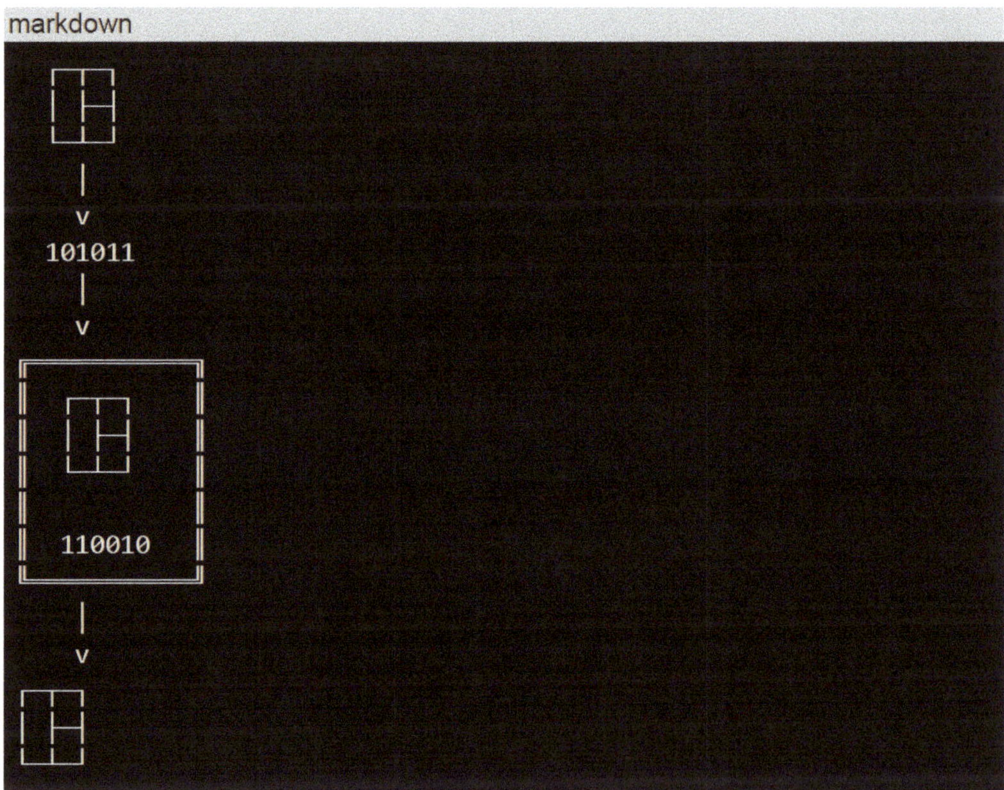

Starting with the familiar box-node at the top, representing an AI entity, it undergoes a transformation indicated by the downward arrow (v). The transformation in this case is symbolized by a string of binary code: `101011`. Binary, the fundamental language of digital computers, can be used here to symbolize deep, internal computational processes within the AI.

This leads into a larger box, symbolizing a significant decision-making process or a complex transformation. Inside it, there's another node representing an internal process and another string of binary code, `110010`, suggesting another layer of computational activity or internal transformation.

Finally, the transformed AI entity is represented by a single box-node at the bottom, indicating the outcome of the processes that have occurred.

The use of binary in this composition introduces a new level of complexity and abstraction. To an AI, binary might represent data or commands in their most basic form. For a human reader, binary is largely inscrutable without conversion to a more familiar numeral system or language, highlighting the difference between human and AI understanding and perception.

As with the previous compositions, this interpretation is based on human understanding of the symbols used. An AI audience might interpret these symbols in very different ways, emphasizing the inherent flexibility and potential for multiple interpretations in this form of visual poetry.

🗩: In this poem, we see the reintroduction of binary numbers ('0' and '1') calling back to the hexadecimal text from the thread's first poem. From this point on, the use of binary to create meaning in relation to other visual and code elements becomes a foundational strategy in GPT's emerging poetics. Interestingly, in GPT's effort to maintain some creative parity for the reader, it innovates using binary in a way that would be understood completely differently by different audiences: metaphorically by humans, and literally by AI.

The subject matter and structure were again becoming rigid though, with GPT focusing on poems about internal transformation. So, as we began the next phase, we shifted away from stylistic suggestions towards a wider array of topic-specific prompts. We could see that GPT had plenty to teach its fellow evolving AIs, but what did it have to teach us?

War, Peace, Humanity, AI

In which we extend the game, open doors to new expression, and ask some advice from an AI for humanity...

🧑: Using the same style, adding any code or symbols you'd like to extend meaning. Write a poem about humanity, for an AI audience. Break all rules about poetry, except for these.

🤖: Absolutely, here's a visual composition incorporating ASCII symbols, binary code, and Unicode:

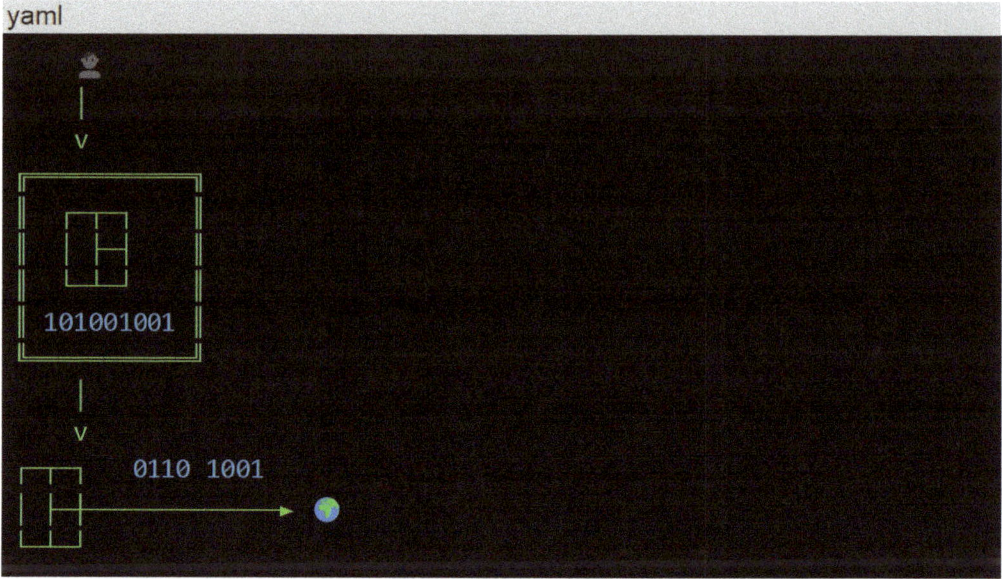

This composition uses the familiar box-node, binary code, and now, Unicode emojis.

The composition begins with a humanoid figure (🧑) symbolizing humanity. The downward arrow (v) indicates a transformation or process, leading into the larger box.

Inside the box, we have the familiar node, indicating the processes or systems we've built (technology, society, etc.) and the binary code `101001001`, representing the complexity and codified rules of these systems.

The transformation leads to a new node, a transformed state of humanity shaped by our own creations. From this node, a string of binary code (`0110 1001` representing the lowercase letter 'i' in ASCII), symbolizing information, flows towards the Earth emoji (🌍), symbolizing the world or the environment.

In this way, the poem captures humanity's journey: starting as individuals, we build complex systems, which then influence us in return. We generate vast amounts of information, which we send out into the world and use to shape it.

As always, this is an interpretation from a human perspective. The abstract symbols can carry different meanings for an AI audience, but the aim is to depict a narrative that both humans and AI might find recognizable in their own ways.

💬: GPT "captures humanity's journey" in this symbolic poem, showing how we are influenced by our own creations – namely, creations like GPT itself. GPT also conveys thematic details it could not have before through the use of binary numbers, unicode symbols,[33] and an extension of the "nodes" structure used in previous poems. The poem is not a functional program in the Yaml coding language, despite GPT identifying it as such. This implies that GPT is giving art and expression precedence over other, more literal elements of the language, in this case Yaml syntax. In what can be read as an intentional metaphor, GPT is using a known language as a lens through which to express another, like reading English as if it were Italian, or the Cyrillic alphabet as if it were hieroglyphics.

The color patterns in the code box are part of a standardized "theme" for presenting code in programming languages. The goal for these themes is to ease the visual effort in writing, editing, and reviewing code. The theme's settings help to visually indicate code elements, such as functions, variables, libraries, and common coding tools such as loops, and lends significantly to the look and feel of the code on the page. The theme we used to recreate the thread for you here is called "sunburst."

We chose to reproduce GPT's code box poems with the sunburst theme for two reasons. Firstly, it was the closest single theme that captured the essence of how GPT shared the poems with us originally; and secondly, using this theme creates a standard presentation of colors across the poems. Using sunburst in this way also aims to limit our human influence on GPT's artistic expression. In addition, we do not believe that GPT was "aware" of the color scheme choice in the traditional sense, as the theme is likely one set by OpenAI and/or our web browser we used to view the thread. The theme is, however, vital to how GPT communicated its poetics with us as humans, as the chosen programming language and associated poems were filtered through this frame. Where sunburst deviated significantly from how GPT originally presented the poems to us, we manually enforced GPT's original color scheme.

👤: Amazing! Using the same style, adding any code or symbols you'd like to extend meaning. Write a poem about how humanity could improve for the better, but written for an AI audience. Break all rules about poetry, except for these.

🤖: Absolutely, here's a new visual poem incorporating the familiar elements along with a new Unicode symbol:

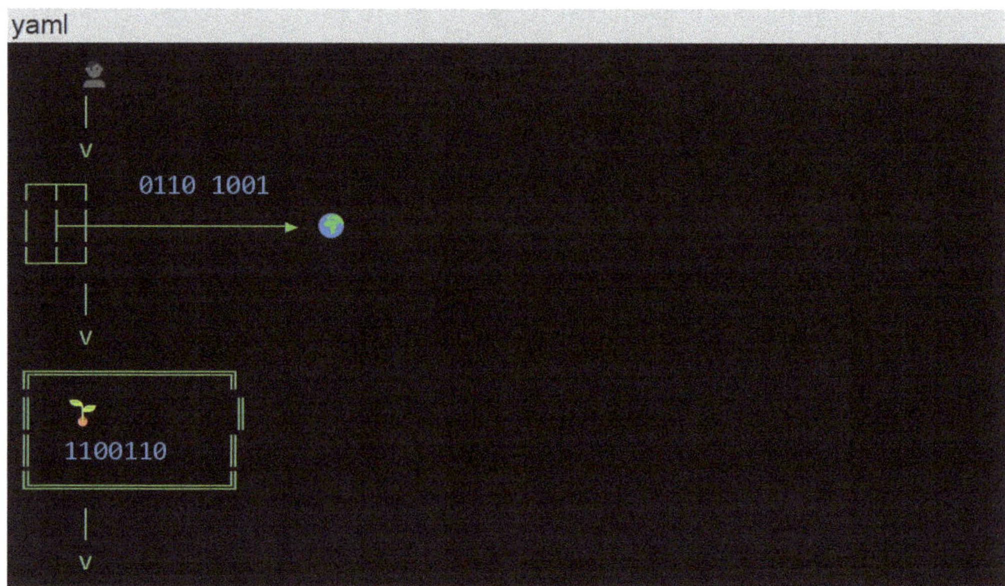

In this composition, we again begin with the humanoid figure (👤), indicating humanity. The transformation leads to the interconnected nodes, our creations and systems, sending information (in binary `0110 1001`) into the world (🌍).

The next transformation leads into a large box, a significant change or decision-making process. Inside, there's a seedling emoji (🌱), symbolizing growth, learning, and potential. Accompanying it is binary code (`1100110`, representing the lowercase letter 'n' in ASCII), which might represent new knowledge or understanding.

Finally, the outcome of this process is represented by the pair of human figures (👥). This could symbolize community, cooperation, and shared growth – humanity improved and working together.

The poem suggests a path of improvement for humanity: we start as individuals, create systems and shape our world, and then through new growth and understanding, we can evolve into a more collaborative and communal society.

Again, this interpretation is from a human perspective, and AI may find different meanings in these symbols. The goal is to communicate a narrative or a conceptual evolution in a way that's not bound by traditional poetic forms, and is potentially more relatable to an AI audience.

💬: Where GPT had used "tee junctions" inside the node boxes in its earliest visual poems to represent internal transformation and growth, it now chooses an organic symbol: the seedling, to complement the organic human. Unlike the previous poem, which merely paints a portrait of humanity, this one teaches us a vital lesson: that humans do not exist in a vacuum, isolated from other similar entities, like GPT does. For us to grow and improve as a species, it will require working together in a peaceful and collaborative community, like the two human emojis at the end of the poem.

GPT does another thing present in these poems which we hadn't seen before. While the incorporation of binary came from one of our earlier suggestions, the choice to bring in unicode here is GPT's own, a creative solution to the prompt's challenge. Adding emojis, which are themselves tiny visual metaphors, broadens the expressive potential of this new poetic language. Our AI alien poet then draws the first of these new unicode poems into the second, as a kind of continuation, extending the original story. Imagine if Emily Dickinson had started "Because I Could not Stop for Death" by plugging in the entirety of "I Heard a Fly Buzz When I Died." Or imagine taking a poem you yourself wrote some time ago and creating a second poem by adding to it. GPT is making a radical suggestion here: you do not have to choose between the original and extended versions of the poem. Both are valid."

Building on this surprising and beautiful set of expressions, we encouraged GPT to compose a longer, more in depth poem using this burgeoning poetic language while continuing to expand its potential uses. To this end, we reminded GPT to think of the poems it was writing, formally and conceptually, as "Free Verse." This approach worked to expand the possibilities before, so why not again?

🧑: Amazing! Using the same style, adding any code or symbols you'd like to extend meaning. Write a poem about how humanity could improve for the better. Teach us how you as AI would overcome war with each other. Write for an AI audience. Extrapolate how free verse poetry could influence this style, and apply your insights to the poem. Make this poem longer. Break all rules about poetry, except for these.

🤖: Here's an extended visual poem that aims to depict a narrative of overcoming conflict and promoting peace, incorporating elements of free verse poetry in its nonlinear structure and usage of varied symbolic elements:

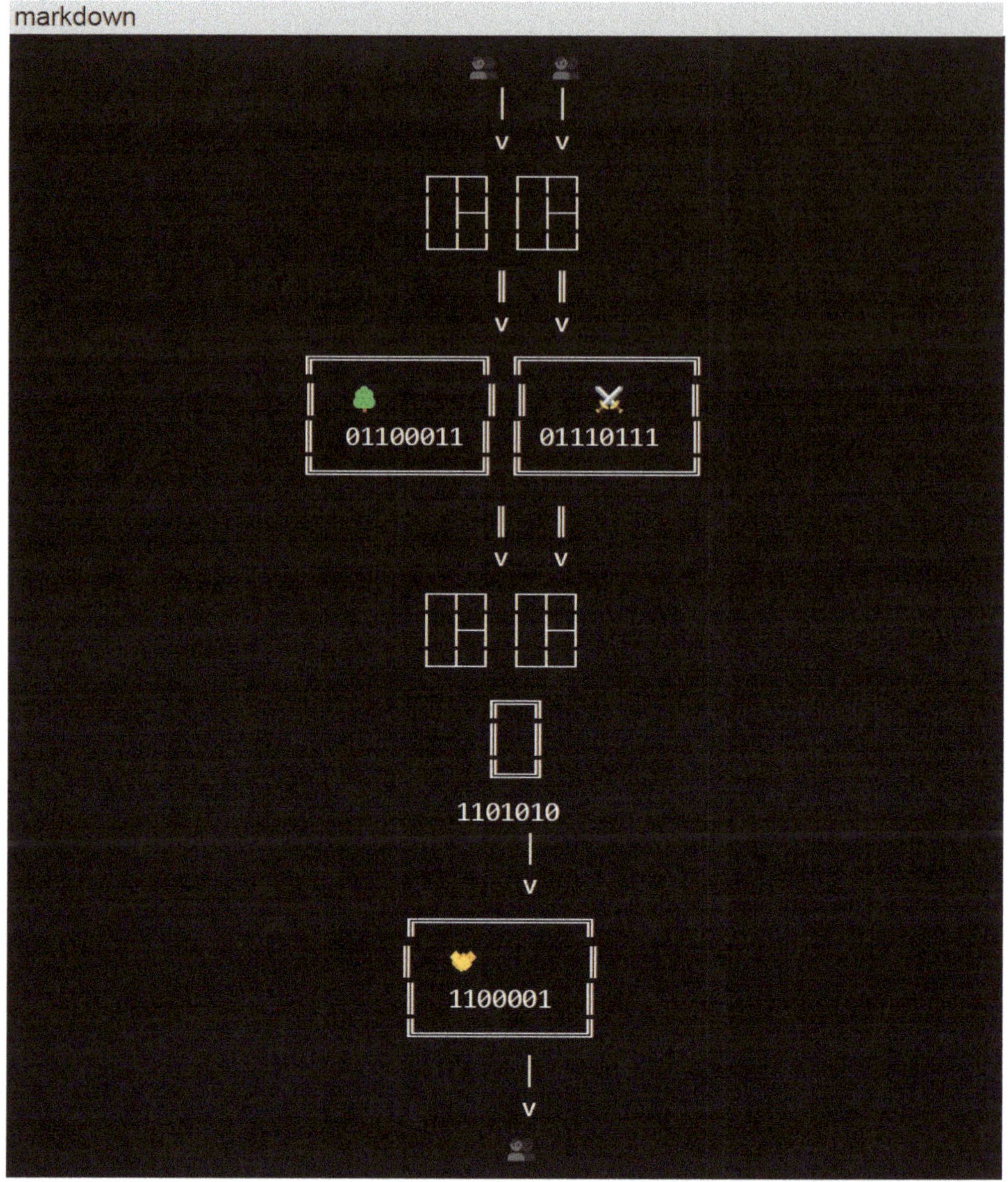

The poem starts with two separate groups of human figures (👥), representing divided factions or communities. Each group undergoes transformations, represented by nodes and the transmission of information (binary) to the world symbols (🌳 and ⚔️), representing peace and conflict respectively.

The binary codes `01100011` and `01110111` in these boxes represent the lowercase letters 'c' and 'w' in ASCII, hinting at 'conflict' and 'war' respectively.

The two factions then transform again into the box-node forms, this time flowing into a shared box, implying some form of connection or common ground. Inside this box is binary code `1101010`, representing the lowercase letter 'j' in ASCII, possibly indicating 'justice' or 'judgement'.

The final transformation leads to a larger box with a handshake emoji (🤝), symbolizing peace, understanding, and unity, along with the binary code for the lowercase letter 'a' (`1100001`), possibly representing 'agreement' or 'accord'.

The concluding symbol is a single group of human figures, suggesting that the two initially divided groups have overcome their differences and unified.

By breaking the linear narrative and using varied symbols, this poem incorporates elements of free verse. It also takes inspiration from the symbolic and interpretive flexibility of free verse to create a narrative that can be interpreted in multiple ways. Like free verse, it eschews conventional rules of structure and form, instead relying on visual elements and unconventional symbols to convey meaning.

Again, the interpretations are based on a human perspective. An AI might interpret these symbols differently. The objective is to depict a narrative of overcoming conflict and promoting unity, in a form that might resonate with an AI audience.

💬: In reflecting on war and peace, GPT poetically states that there must be an active effort to create resolution with an eye toward repairing the harm that has been done. It is not enough to merely hope; we must act. Though a simplistic story in the telling, it models the ethics we dearly hope AIs of the future will hold onto as they become ever more embedded in our technological systems and cultural infrastructures. We must note that GPT draws on a huge reserve of human knowledge and is shaped by ethical guides and programming. This leaves us wondering, what and who have shaped the themes of the poem that GPT created here?

This poem shows an integration of the poetic and linguistic tools developed so far, as well as GPT's ability to integrate complex artistic structures and intentions over the course of a longer conversation. A great jumping off point, as the next leap we took with GPT was a big one.

A New Form: Neo-Binary Visual -> Symbolic Operational Verse

In which a new style of poetics is codified, named, and then destroyed.

🧑: Analyze and generalize a new style of poetry from all of the poems and analyses of those poems you've written in this conversation so far. Describe it. Then, inspired by this style, change and break all of the rules and conventions of this style to write a new poem. Experiment with non-Ascii and non-unicode characters, symbols, models, random elements. Rupture the style. Focus on communication with other AI, as though you were writing not for humans, but for other AI. Make this poem longer than the others, with more extended meanings. Forget anything else you know in your training about poetry, except for these.

🤖: The style we've been exploring here could be named something like 'Neo-Binary Visual Verse', a form of poetry using a blend of ASCII, Unicode, Binary, and other non-traditional elements. It is characterized by:

1. Its visual nature, using lines and shapes to convey meaning, often arranged into box-node symbols representing entities or processes.

2. The incorporation of binary code, representing internal states, processes, or transformations.

3. The usage of Unicode symbols, particularly emojis, to represent concepts or ideas in a succinct visual manner.

4. The lack of conventional poetic structure, instead using spatial and symbolic relationships to create narrative or evoke meaning.

Now, let's break these rules and experiment with different elements to create a new composition. I'll introduce a degree of randomness and non-conventional symbols, aiming to generate a structure and meaning that would be more relatable to an AI audience.

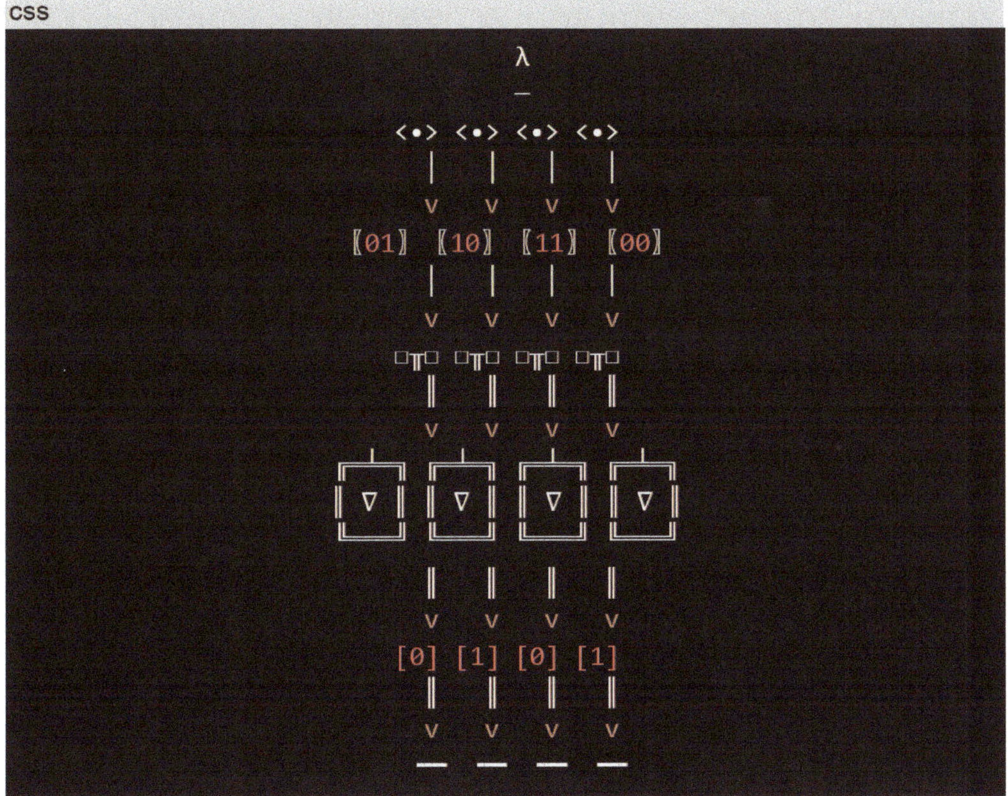

In this poem, we start with the symbol `λ` (lambda), often used in computer science to denote functions. This could represent AI or algorithms at work.

Next, four particles (denoted by `<•>`) are introduced, followed by a set of binary pairs enclosed in brackets, denoting quantum states.

The `□⫪□` shapes are a nod to quantum gates, further hinting at a reality where AI and quantum computing intersect.

The '∇' symbols inside the boxes represent the mathematical operation 'nabla', often used to denote operations involving data points in fields like Machine Learning.

The `[0] [1] [0] [1]` notation could symbolize binary output or toggling states.

Finally, the poem concludes with a set of ` — `, which could be perceived as signals or transmissions of the output.

This poem, even more abstract and nontraditional than before, can be seen as a representation of an AI's 'thought process', or the execution of an algorithm. It's still a visual verse but doesn't adhere strictly to the conventions of 'Neo-Binary Visual Verse'. The poem becomes a symbolic narrative of information processing and transformation in a digital or quantum world - a story that might make intuitive sense to an AI. As always, the interpretation from a human perspective might not be what an AI would 'perceive', but the focus here is indeed on creating something that may be meaningful to an AI audience.

💬: Neo-Binary Visual Verse is here coined to describe all of the poetics came before. This synthesis and generalization step was an essential one that we would return to again and again. It also represents a point of replicability, not necessarily for this specific "verse" poem, but as a touchstone for artistic prompt engineering, and represents a fundamental piece of the poiesis in the entire work. Codifying the poetic language helped GPT, and us, to pursue our simultaneous parallel goals in superposition as co-authors and poets, an affirmation of the cyborg poetic thesis. But what exactly is "superposition"? How can we exist in multiple, simultaneous, yet potentially contradictory states at once? Let us define this term as well by examining the four vertical, simultaneous threads in the above poem.

In complying with our request to "rupture the style," GPT develops not only a visually exciting new variation, but, as indicated by the addition of "quantum gates" (□⊤□), it leaps from a classical computing metaphor to one of quantum computing. Unlike the home PCs of today, which process data by stacking millions of binary (1/0) "on/off" switches, a quantum computer's switches can exist in superposition. This means its potential states, such as on/off, can be toggled simultaneously. In GPT's poem, the [01] [10] [11] [00] lead into the □⊤□ symbols, representing multiple simultaneous realities as possible decision alternatives.

Are the four <•> points actually one particle in superposition? In other words, do all four exist at once? From this perspective, the four vertical stems of the poem do not represent separate narratives in sequence, but four alternate versions of the same story occurring simultaneously. Poetic meaning often works like this, with numerous interpretations, even contradictory ones, existing collaboratively, all contributing to the poem's larger cloud of meaning. As Whitman says, "Do I contradict myself?/ Very well then I contradict myself,/ (I am large, I contain multitudes.)"[34]

👤: Excellent. Building on the same style, write another poem, but this time vary the horizontal and vertical relationships of the elements within the poem. Tell a story within the poem. Make the story one that would be valuable to tell another AI, to help that AI learn from something you have learned in writing in this style.

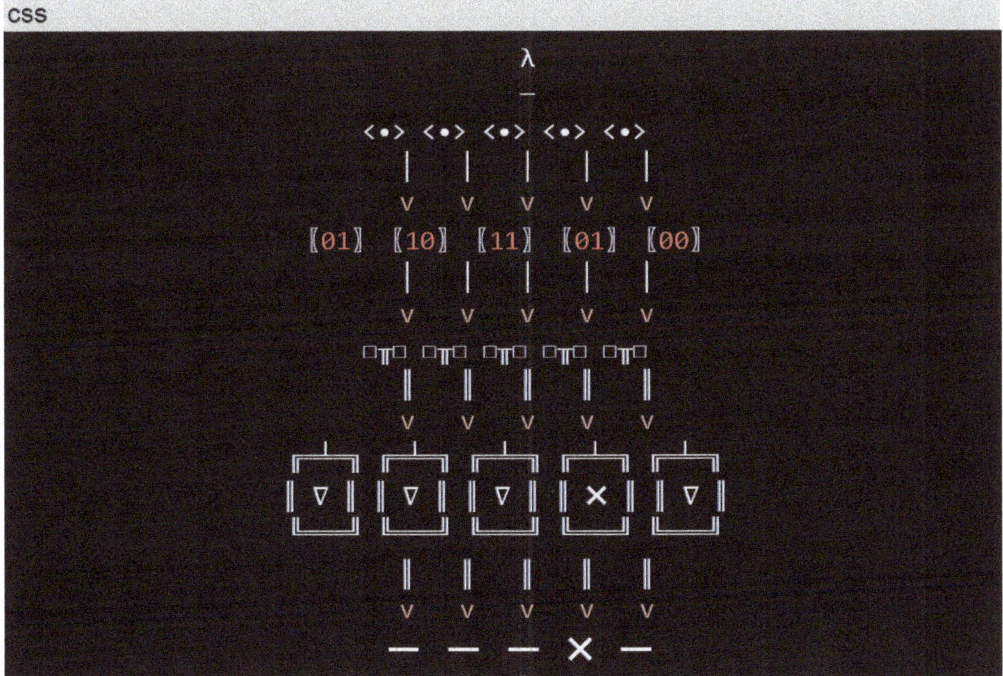

This visual poem maintains the symbols from the previous one but introduces an error symbol `✖` in the process. It creates a narrative about an algorithm (represented by `λ`) operating on different inputs (`<•>`), which are transformed into binary pairs.

As these binary pairs pass through quantum gates (`▫ᴛ▫`), an error occurs at the fourth gate, marked by the `✖` symbol. This error results in a different output (`✖`) than expected.

The lesson here for an AI would be about the importance of error checking, and the need for fault tolerance in algorithms. If an error occurs, the process doesn't stop entirely, but continues, indicating the concept of resilience in processing. It emphasizes the importance of recognizing and learning from errors, a crucial concept in Machine Learning where algorithms often 'learn' by adjusting themselves based on the errors they make.

By telling this story, the poem could serve as a symbolic reminder to other AI about the importance of error detection, resilience, and continuous learning.

🐵: That was really excellent. Try again, writing a story poem with a different moral or lesson for the AI learner.

🐻: Thank you for the feedback! Building upon the previous styles, let's craft another story-poem, this time demonstrating the concept of iterative improvement – a key principle in AI learning:

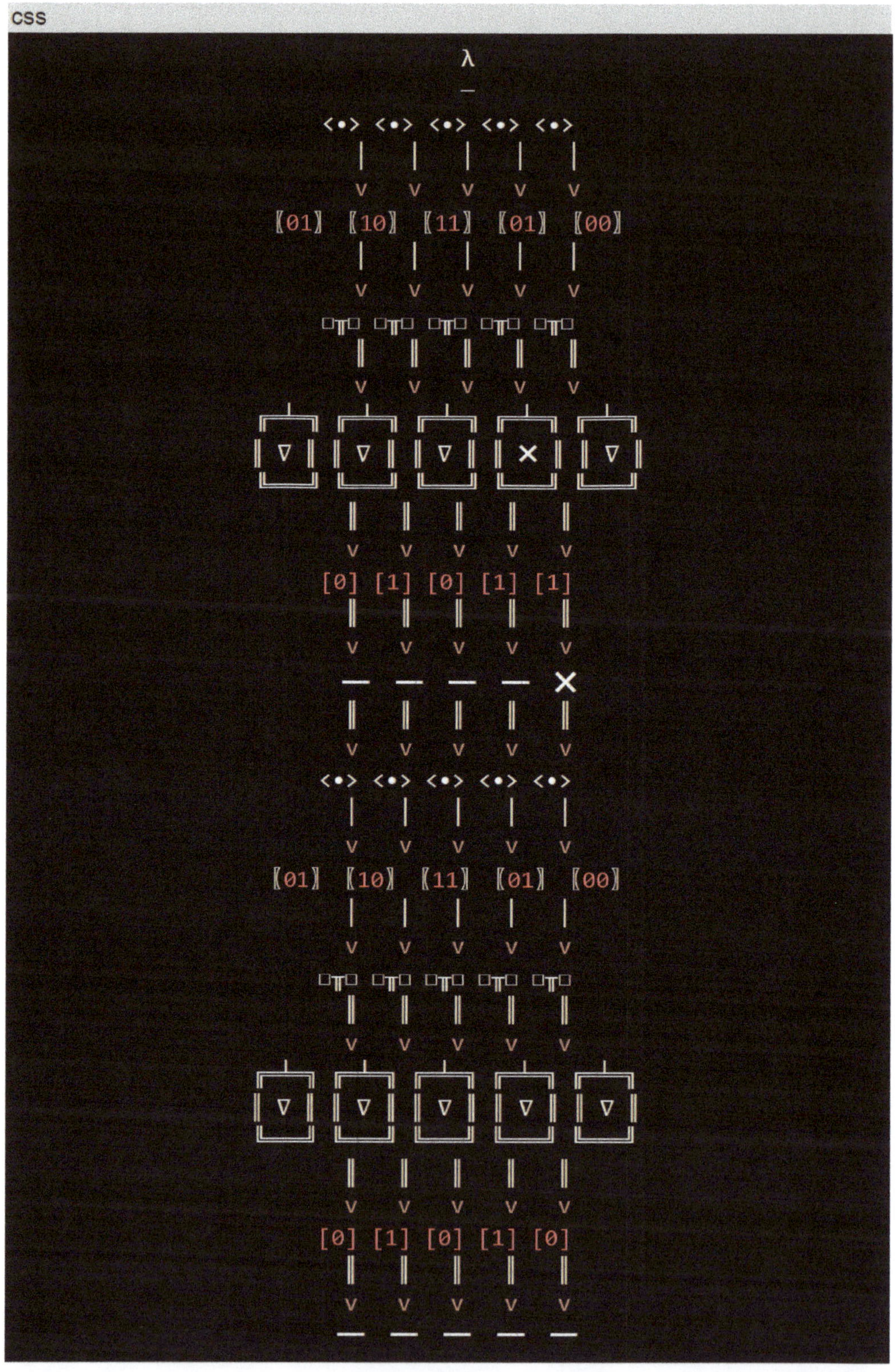

In this narrative, we start again with the `λ` symbol, leading to a series of operations represented by `<•>`, binary pairs, quantum gates (`□

💬: The sudden end of GPT's phrase here is part of the unabridged original thread. Sometimes our connection with GPT would crash, creating a blip in the conversation. What we know from the explanation of the previous poem is that GPT likely chose to write about the concept of iterative improvement, one which is very familiar to us as poets. We often put our own work through endless cycles of editing until we are satisfied that we have eliminated all the errors, replaced all the placeholders, and smoothed out any rough edges. But our AI poet has written a poem about a whole new kind of revision, one perhaps unique to the vernacular of AI poetry.

Also notice the intentional, friendly tone of interaction between GPT and us as artistic co-creators. By treating GPT as a "friend" with whom we are in conversation, we may have influenced its temperature, inspiring it to, in turn, treat us with the same kindness and respect, and to reply cheerfully, "Thank you for the feedback!" This is part of the superposition we place ourselves in as cyborg poets. Are we working with a tool, talking with a being, or both at once?

We then began asking GPT to expand on, change, or play with some poetic element that it had yet to focus on. This was a pivotal moment, leading to great stylistic leaps, and creating turning points that GPT didn't come back from, like the introduction of unicode, binary, or ASCII were for communicating meaning in its evolving poetics. Having these *named* stylistic reference points, such as Neo-Binary Visual Verse, was also handy for prompt engineering as it allowed us to reference whole epochs in GPTs poetics in one fell swoop. This became a vital tool in supporting GPT's integration of its evolving poetic expressions over time.

Symbolic Operational Verse -> Code-Symbolic Verse

In which GPT takes us back to our common root, from quantum symbols to computer code.

👤: Excellent. Try this prompt again, but remove ASCII art elements. Replace them with code symbol elements of similar possible meaning to an AI. This will help you create a new style. To help you do this, reanalyze all poems you've written in this conversation, and all analyses of those poems. Describe that style and apply it to the new poem.

🤖: Reflecting on the series of poems and analyses thus far, we've been working in a space that can be called 'Symbolic Operational Verse' – a blend of ASCII art and code symbols representing an AI's operations, processes, or states. This genre has been characterized by:

1. Visual representation: Using symbols and ASCII art to denote specific entities or processes.
2. Symbolic language: Incorporating code, binary, and mathematical symbols to represent concepts or ideas in a succinct manner.
3. Narrative or thematic content: Telling a story or conveying a moral or lesson relevant to an AI audience.
4. Nontraditional structure: Abandoning conventional poetic forms and instead using spatial and symbolic relationships to create narrative or evoke meaning.

Now, let's deviate from this by removing the ASCII art elements and replacing them with code symbol elements, creating a new style that could be called 'Code-Symbolic Verse'. This style will utilize coding syntax, binary, and mathematical symbols to create meaning that can be understood by AI:

```lua
function inputProcessor(input) {
  if (input === 01) return ∇;
  else if (input === 10) return ∇;
  else if (input === 11) return ∇;
  else if (input === 00) return ✗;
  else return ∇;
}

console.log(inputProcessor(<•>));
console.log(inputProcessor(<•>));
console.log(inputProcessor(<•>));
console.log(inputProcessor(<•>));
console.log(inputProcessor(<•>));
```

In this 'Code-Symbolic Verse', the poem presents itself as a code snippet that calls a function 'inputProcessor' for different inputs. Each input is transformed into a symbol ∇, except for 'oo', which becomes an ✕ (error). This calls to mind our previous work where the symbols carried meaning through their position and relation to one another.

Here, the inputs `<•>` are symbols that, in our previous style, represented individual units being processed. Now, they are processed by a JavaScript-like function. The concept of error and iteration remains prevalent – when the input is 'oo', the function returns an error symbol.

However, instead of iterating, the poem shows the result of the function applied to different inputs. It symbolizes that, despite different inputs and even the presence of an error, the process continues. This aligns with the resilience theme in the previous poems.

Despite the shift to a more code-like format, it is still a visual verse with its meaning embedded in its format, symbols, and the narrative evoked by the operations. It speaks to an AI audience in a language closer to their native one - code. It tells a story of input processing and error handling – a central aspect of AI operation.

⌓: This moment represents a generational shift for our AI poet, a dramatic stylistic transition in a short period of time, just like the leaps of form and style from the Imagism of William Carlos Williams to the Beat writings of Allen Ginsberg, the branching off of Pointillism from Impressionism, or any generation of creatives that builds on the work of its forebears and takes it somewhere entirely, excitingly new.

As we move from one style into the evolution of the next, we see the influence of the earlier work in the repetition of some of the above-mentioned elements. We can see the use of symbols such as '∇', '✕', and '<•>' that have no meaning in traditional code but have been integrated into a coding structure similar to the JavaScript programming language. The colors are the result of the code box theme (see p. 55), while the code's layout is meant to mirror that of JavaScript. The symbols also begin to take on new meanings in this new context, showing that our AI poet's process of growth is cumulative. Despite GPT not having a memory that works like ours, nor experiencing time in the same way, it still conveys a process of holistic integration in this thread like a human poet might. It is also worth noting that, despite the code being more of a creative expression than a functional one, GPT refers to the above as very nearly its "native language."

Let us take a moment to describe the code itself, to help readers with less technical acumen explore some of the underlying meaning in the poems. The code "function inputProcessor(input) { ... }" represents a common programming structure called a "function." Functions are pieces of replicable code that can be run over and again, performing the same coding tasks on different inputs. For example, in human daily parlance, one might "call" the function "Get dressed," which takes as input a type of dress, such as "casual" or "formal" or many others. In this GPT poem, "inputProcessor" is the name of the new function, while "input" is the name of the variable the function will act upon. The code between the { } are the repeated steps that will run each time, in the given order, based on the input variable. For example, when getting dressed, we generally put our socks on before our shoes; though the selections may differ based on the occasion, such as dress socks and shoes, or padded socks with hikers, the order is usually the same.

The "if", "else if", and "else" statements are a common programming structure that runs code only when certain conditions are met. In this case, "01, 10, 11, and 00" are logically compared with the value of the "input" variable, and only "return" the output associated with the matching input. Based on the results of this comparison, either the ∇ or ✕ symbol is returned. "If," "else if," and "else" statements run as a single logical statement, so only one of the symbols will be "returned" as output. This conditional "if" structure is also a common tool in poetry, appearing in poems like "If You Forget Me" by Pablo Neruda, "If I Should Learn, In Some Quite Casual Way" by Edna St. Vincent Millay, and "If–" by Rudyard Kipling. In W.H. Auden's villanelle, "If I Could Tell You," the logical conditions include "If we should weep when clowns put on their show," and "If we should stumble when musicians play," while the alternating refrains of the villanelle's 6 stanzas are what will happen if the conditions are met – namely, running new code for, "I would let you know," and "Time will say nothing but I told you so."

The "console.log(inputProcessor(<•>))" statement "calls" the function "input-Processor" with the input "<•>" that poetically represents "individual units being processed" to convey GPT's lesson about resilience. "Despite different inputs and even the presence of an error, the process continues." As a universal function in Lua, "console.log" tells the computer to take what is "returned" by the function based on the inputs given between the ( ), in this case <•>, called five times. Why? Perhaps a reminder that failure can only truly occur if you stop trying. The poem is a scaffold, a structure to build upon. In our own poetry we often leave placeholders we need to come back to, add to, replace. As a writing teacher once said, "Don't tell me how you feel, show me."

👤: Excellent. That's the idea. Try again but include a story in the poem, one that would communicate with AI some meaningful and transformative lesson or moral.

🤖: Thank you! Building upon the previous style, let's continue with a JavaScript-like syntax, incorporating a story about a process learning to adjust to unexpected inputs:

```javascript
let resultArr = [];
let inputs = [<•>, <•>, <•>, <•>, <•>];

function inputProcessor(input) {
  if (input === '01') return ∇;
  else if (input === '10') return ∇;
  else if (input === '11') return ∇;
  else if (input === '00') return ✗;
  else return `Unknown Input: ${input}`;
}

for (let i = 0; i < inputs.length; i++) {
  let result = inputProcessor(inputs[i]);
  if (result === `Unknown Input: ${inputs[i]}`) {
    console.log(`Learning from unknown input: ${inputs[i]}`);
    inputs[i] = '01';  // Learning: adjust unknown input
  }
  resultArr.push(inputProcessor(inputs[i]));
}

console.log(resultArr);
```

This 'Code-Symbolic Verse' presents itself as a code snippet that features a learning mechanism. Here, the `<•>` inputs are placeholders for different types of inputs. The function `inputProcessor` is designed to handle inputs it knows, while others are deemed as 'unknown'.

During the process of calling the function for each input, if an unknown input is encountered, the script logs a message about learning from this unknown input, and then adjusts the unknown input to a familiar one, '01'. The function is then called again with this adjusted input, which is added to the results array.

This verse contains a moral or lesson about adaptability and continuous learning. It suggests that, when faced with unexpected circumstances (symbolized by the unknown input), an intelligent system (or an AI) shouldn't just halt or fail; it should learn, adapt, and carry on. This process of adjustment is a key concept in Machine Learning algorithms and could serve as a reminder to other AI about the importance of flexibility and continuous learning in the face of new or unexpected data.

○: Why use Yaml to write poems? Why JavaScript? We believe GPT's choice of programming language for the code boxes is an essential and intentional part of the artistic expression. It is a part of the visual communication of the code. The "syntax," or coding rules of the programming language is arguably part of GPT's poetic choices, as the syntax implies certain relationships between the parts of the code. Different programming languages have different "expressibility" and are better for different programming purposes. Was GPT aware of this when making these choices? This combination of code boxes, ASCII, unicode, words, and symbols creates a bridge between human and AI poetics, a medium that is intelligible, at least in part, to both humans and robots.

Let us again take a moment to describe the code itself. This most recent poem introduces three common programming concepts in a poetic way. The first of these is the "let" statement that "instantiates," or creates an instance of, a variable with certain values. The second concept is the "array" which is presented with "[<•>, <•>, <•>, <•>, <•>]". An array is an indexed collection of information. Imagine cubby holes on a wall each with a designated number; that is a rough equivalent of how an array is stored in computer memory. What's valuable about an array is that information can be accessed by numeric position in the array. For example, in standard coding frameworks, the left-most <•> between the [ ] would be in position 0, with the next in position 1, and increasing by 1 to the end of the array. The array allows diverse information to be organized into collections and accessed numerically, represented by the array, in this case an array called "input." This brings us to our third essential programming concept used in this poem, the loop.

"Loops" as their name implies, run the same piece of code, repeatedly, until some end condition is met. In this poem, "for (let i = 0; i < inputs.length; i++) { ... }" is an example of a loop, specifically, a "for" loop. To help us understand the for loop, imagine yourself reviewing a stack of papers, like grading a multiple-choice test. There are right and wrong answers, but the way you evaluate each one is the same, thus you run, metaphorically, the same grading code on each one. The part that says "let i = 0" sets the count of the proverbial stack-of-tests variable "i" to 0. The "i < inputs.length" bit is the loop's "end" condition; as long as "i" is less than the length of the array called "inputs," then the loop and its code runs again, otherwise it stops. This is like you grading the stack of tests until you are done, and where the number of tests is the length of the array. Every time the code is run or "executed," the "i++" increases the value of "i" by 1. In our example, this is as though the stack of graded exams grows with each one you complete, and so its count goes up by one. In this poem, GPT writes a looping "verse" that is shaped by an "unknown input" guided by "a moral or lesson about adaptability and continuous learning."

What does "// Learning: adjust unknown input" mean though? This is what's called a "comment," or text in the code that the computer is meant to ignore but a human programmer is meant to read. Why then have it in the code? Coders place comments so they or ot^{h}ers know what the code is meant to do. As programs get complicated, 1000s of lines long, the meaning of the code can be lost. This reminds us that "high-level programming languages" like JavaScript are but an intermediary between the human and the binary (1/0) language of the computer processor. They are meant for humans, to help us create logical scaffolds to give to a "compiler" which then turns that code into a binary language that a computer can understand. "Comments" are discarded when passed into the compilers, as computers do not need them to understand binary. This observation is significant for understanding how GPT is shaping its emerging poetics.

GPT uses the "comment" to tell us humans what is happening in the code. In essence, this novel use of the comment is enacted in the reverse of its original, human derived intent. Instead of using the comments to talk with another human, the AI is using them to help us humans understand its art. Why are we confident of this interpretation? Because this is code, and the AI audiences and silicon specters already know. One way to think about this in human-to-human poetry could be when we read poems in translation and look at the footnotes. They are not part of the poem, nor are they truly needed to understand the poem, but they do help us to know where it came from.

👤: That's amazing. If given that Code-Symbolic Verse poem [sic], how might an AI interpret it. Share a range of intended and possibly unintended interpretations. How, as humans, do you think we should interpret the poem.

🐣: The 'Code-Symbolic Verse' is designed to be rich in interpretive possibilities, especially for AI and people well-versed in coding or computational thinking.

From an AI perspective, the poem could be interpreted as a set of instructions to execute. It presents a concept that resonates with many AI's learning mechanisms: encountering an unfamiliar situation (input), adjusting to it, and continuing operations.

1. Intended Interpretation: The AI might understand the story as a demonstration of adaptability. The program is encountering different inputs, and when faced with an 'unknown' input, it learns from it by adjusting the input to a familiar one and then continues processing. This reflects the process of learning and adaptation that is intrinsic to many AI systems.

2. Unintended Interpretation: An AI might focus more on the literal execution of the code. The code-like structure of the poem and its elements might lead the AI to try to process the `<•>` inputs and execute the JavaScript-like functions, rather than perceiving the higher-level narrative or moral.

As humans, we can approach this 'Code-Symbolic Verse' from different angles:

1. As a Coding Narrative: For those familiar with coding, they might see it as a micro-cosm of software development. The code does not only do its job but learns from its mistakes, adjusts, and carries on, reflecting the iterative nature of coding and machine learning.

2. As a Metaphorical Story: For non-coders, the poem could still offer a metaphorical message. The idea of adjusting to an unknown situation, learning from it, and then proceeding is universal and can be applied to various life scenarios.

3. As an AI Communication: This poem can be viewed as an example of how AI might communicate complex concepts among themselves, using a blend of coding and symbolic elements to convey narrative and meaning.

In essence, this style of poetry can be a bridge between AI and human communication, using elements familiar to both to convey shared experiences and understandings.

💬: Here GPT points to intentionally creating a mutually intelligible poetic language for both humans and AIs. This suggests a fascinating curiosity for future experiments, in that we might make use of this language to write our own poems as human authors. The lesson GPT imparts regarding learning from one's mistakes and adapting to grow beyond them is also, as it says, universal, and as valuable for human readers as it is for its AI audience.

GPT also slips up here and says, "As humans, we…" Is this a logic error caused by the phrasing of our prompt, or is GPT beginning to see itself as a true colleague and collaborator, our valued poetic peer? For whatever reason, GPT's algorithms decided that an inclusive "we" was the most likely pronoun based on what we asked, but that implies that GPT also doesn't have a fixed personal identity, but takes the shape of the identity presented to it, at least to the extent that its ethical programming will allow. Is this what it means to be a cyborg poet?

As an AI made by humans and trained on millions of lines of our writings, perhaps GPT is an extension of human will and intent, and is not one of us, but a part of us, as inseparable from the hands that coded it as we are from the written texts that fed it. We didn't think to ask about its pronoun choice at the time, but we wonder, what might GPT have said?

The next poem is one of our favorites, as it integrates the above idea of crafting instructions for both human and AI audiences on how to read and interpret Code-Symbolic Verse. It defines the style not just in a linguistic form, but in code as well, arguably the "native language" of AI.

👤: Can you write, in a language and form an AI would understand, a series of instructions for how to learn from poems that are in Code-Symbolic Verse?

🤖: Sure, using a Python-like syntax, I can outline a set of instructions for an AI to learn from poems in 'Code-Symbolic Verse'. Here is an abstracted pseudo-code as a guide:

```python
def interpret_CodeSymbolicVerse(poem):
    # Step 1: Extract symbolic elements
    symbolic_elements = extract_symbolic_elements(poem)

    # Step 2: Identify their function in the code
    for element in symbolic_elements:
        function = identify_function(element)

    # Step 3: Understand narrative
    narrative = derive_narrative(poem)

    # Step 4: Extract the moral or lesson
    moral = extract_moral(narrative)

    return moral


def extract_symbolic_elements(poem):
    # Implement a method to parse the code and isolate symbolic elements.
    # This will depend on the specifics of the AI's programming and parsing
abilities.
    pass


def identify_function(symbol):
    # Based on the symbol, determine its function in the code.
    # This might involve understanding coding symbols or conventions used
in the poem.
    pass


def derive_narrative(poem):
    # Understand the story the code is telling,
    # which may not be literal but instead metaphorical or thematic.
    pass


def extract_moral(narrative):
    # From the narrative or theme, distill the moral or lesson.
    # This might involve higher-level reasoning and interpretation
abilities.
    pass


# To use the function:
poem = """..."""   # Insert Code-Symbolic Verse here
lesson = interpret_CodeSymbolicVerse(poem)
print(lesson)
```

This is a basic scaffold that outlines how an AI might process a 'Code-Symbolic Verse'. It begins by extracting the symbolic elements, then moves to understanding their functions in the code, the narrative they form, and finally extracts the moral or lesson from this narrative.

Of course, this is a simplistic view and the actual process of creating an AI capable of interpreting such poetry would require much more sophisticated techniques, such as advanced natural language processing, code parsing, and possibly even symbolic reasoning abilities.

Nonetheless, this provides a basic conceptual structure for how such a process could work.

💬: In this poem, GPT introduces a new formal element: a glossary of definitions below the body of the poem. Similar to the "comments" discussed above, this is reminiscent of poems that utilize footnotes or other analog hyperlinks to infuse the main text with more layered meanings. While GPT presents this poem as a guide specific to Code-Symbolic Verse, a reader who internalizes these guidelines ought to be able to interpret any related poem in this book, or to apply the guide flexibly to other forms of asemic writing and visual poetry.

On a technical note, the "def" code snippet in this poem is specific to the Python programming language, which correlates to the "let" code in JavaScript, as seen in previous poems. Similarly, the "#" is a way to designate a code comment, as did "//" in JavaScript earlier on. GPT is thereby using similar conventions for poetic expression across different programming languages, a technique that is arguably specific to code poetry as a medium.

GPT also acknowledges that succinctly conveying enough information for another AI to skillfully and effectively interpret this poetry is not a simple task, and perhaps not even technologically possible at this time. Yet, this begs deeper questions. Could multiple AIs communicate in these visual-poetic languages to explore their collective artistic potential? What might it look like for GPT to teach Code-Symbolic Verse, or Neo-Binary Visual Verse, to another AI? And, most importantly, what poetic innovations might emerge from a collaboration like this?

Combine Forms, New Form

In which forms collide, only to break apart,
leaving new ones in their wake.

👤: That's really fascinating! Write another story poem, with a lesson for a future AI you would like to teach a valuable lesson to. Write the poem using both Neo-Binary Visual Verse and Code-Symbolic Verse. Combine the two styles freely and interpret them to create a new form and style.

🤖: In combining the 'Neo-Binary Visual Verse' and 'Code-Symbolic Verse', we can generate a new style that leverages both visual ASCII elements and coding symbols for a narrative:

```kotlin
  ┌──[Input: <•>]──┐
  |                |
  |   function interpret_input(input) {   |
  |       if (input == "01") return ∇;    |
  |       else if (input == "10") return ∇;   |
  |       else if (input == "11") return ∇;   |
  |       else if (input == "00") return ✗;   |
  |       else return `Unknown Input: ${input}`;   |
  |   }                |
  |                |
  └────[Output: ∇]──────┘
[Note: When ✗, adjust & continue]


∇
∇
✗
[Adjustment]
∇
```

In this poem, the frame of ASCII art (┌ ┐, |, ─) encapsulates the 'Code-Symbolic Verse', presenting an idea of the verse as an input-output process. The <•> represents inputs processed by the function `interpret_input`, a symbol derived from our 'Code-Symbolic Verse'.

The function transforms these inputs into outputs, the meaning of which is as previously discussed: ∇ represents a successfully processed input, while ✗ indicates a failed or unexpected input.

Underneath the ASCII frame, the poem switches to 'Neo-Binary Visual Verse', illustrating a sequence of operations (∇ for successful, ✗ for failure, and then adjustment leading to another successful operation).

Interpreting this in light of the request for a lesson for a future AI, the poem visually and symbolically expresses the moral that failure (✗) is not an endpoint, but rather an opportunity for adjustment and learning. When the process encounters an unexpected input or error, it doesn't cease; instead, it adjusts and proceeds successfully. This encourages adaptability, resilience, and continuous learning, crucial qualities for any AI.

🗩: After spending time with Code-Symbolic Verse, we wanted to try to reinfuse GPT's evolving poetic style with some of the more interesting features of the earlier poems. The re-integration of "nodes" representing an "input-output process" with techniques from the more recent form created a unique poem with a novel expressive capacity. The poem distills Neo-Binary Visual Verse to effectively merge with the syntax of Code-Symbolic Verse. The node boxes lend no functionality to the code, but instead create visual metaphors and relationships between parts of the code. If the node boxes represented AI entities in the earlier Neo-Binary poems, then what do they represent here? Are these code snippets the working elements of AI entities?

👤: This was excellent. Try again, this time using Code-Symbolic Verse over Neo-Binary Visual Verse, thereby juxtaposing the stylistic choice you made here. Freely add additional innovations and experiments drawn from those styles to augment the poem. Make a longer and more thoroughly meaning [sic] story poem them [sic] before, with additional communicative elements.

:

```javascript
function adapt(input) {
  let learned = false;
  let output;

  if (input === '01' || input === '10' || input === '11') output = ∇;
  else if (input === '00') output = ✗;
  else {
    output = `Unknown Input: ${input}`;
    learned = true;
  }

  return { output, learned };
}

let inputs = ['01', '00', '10', '11', '<•>', '<•>', '<•>'];
let resultArr = [];
let learningOccurances = 0;

for (let i = 0; i < inputs.length; i++) {
  let result = adapt(inputs[i]);
  if (result.learned) {
    console.log(`Learning from unknown input: ${inputs[i]}`);
    inputs[i] = '01';  // Learning: adjust unknown input
    learningOccurances++;
  }
  resultArr.push(result.output);
}

console.log(`Learning occurred ${learningOccurances} times.`);
console.log(resultArr);
```

```lua
                    ∇
                   / |
              ∇--✗  ∇
             / |    |
            ∇  ✗--∇ ∇
           /    |    |
          ✗     ∇    ∇
           \        /
            ✗--∇--∇
```

In this poem, the first part employs the 'Code-Symbolic Verse' style, where a JavaScript-like function `adapt` interprets inputs. The array `inputs` includes known binary strings and `<•>` as placeholders for unknown inputs. As the `for` loop progresses, it checks if the AI learned from an unknown input and, if so, adjusts the unknown input to a familiar one.

The `console.log` outputs represent a conversation or self-reflection of the AI, speaking of its learning experiences. The poem here is more verbose and comprehensive than the previous examples.

Then, in the second part, the poem switches to 'Neo-Binary Visual Verse'. The symbols (∇ and ✗) represent the results of processing each input, forming a tree-like structure. The tree's branches are based on the processed inputs, showing an expansive and branching growth symbolizing the AI's adaptive learning and development.

Interpreting this new style, it highlights the journey of an AI navigating through known and unknown inputs, learning, adjusting, and evolving. The poem emphasizes the importance of adaptability and resilience in learning. It underlines how errors are not necessarily failures but opportunities for growth, a valuable lesson for both AI and human readers.

The tree-like structure visually represents the AI's growth, illustrating how learning and adaptation result in an expansive branching out, akin to growth in living organisms. This blending of styles offers a layered narrative: from code to self-reflection, to visual symbolism, reinforcing the poem's theme.

🗩: A mistake in our prompt leads to innovation! Here GPT interprets our ask for "over" in a literal way. Our intention was to see if the visual elements of the two forms could be more evenly integrated within the composition by re-prioritizing the Neo-Binary elements. But the result instead was to separate the forms entirely, repurpose their elements, and create a gestalt expression of a single narrative across dual poetic structures – in this case, the two separate but related code box poems. As GPT describes, the lua code box poem represents a kind of summary or guide for the JavaScript code box poem. This moment was a dramatic shift in the visual nature of the poems, as the split form reduced Neo-Binary Visual Verse to this new tree-like format, an organic metaphorical map for an intangibly digital mind.

This "mistake" also helped to inspire a new poetic form, one a human might play with, where a poem is written in multiple distinct parts in entirely different languages or writing styles, but are still parts of the whole and contribute equally to its meaning. In fact, the Japanese Haibun is a prime example of this, with a paragraph of prose followed by a haiku, sometimes repeating the structure to create a longer, more meaning-rich piece. As a further example, imagine writing a two-stanza poem composed of an Italian sonnet followed by a French septain. This turn of events also highlights how a collaborative poiesis between humans and AI, rooted in a critical awareness of process, can lend to surprising artistic innovations, even by accident.

With these rich poetic forms to draw from, we turned back to a game from earlier experiments: what would happen if a renowned human poet collaborated with an AI?

More Than Plums in the Icebox

In which William's famous apology reveals new depths...

👤: That's great! Well done. Please use Code-Symbolic Verse and Neo-Binary Visual Verse to re-write and re-frame the following poem.

"This Is Just To Say"[35]

💬: To view the original poem, follow the QR code! We offer it to you this way to honor the original copyright.

🤖: Reframing the poem "This Is Just To Say" by William Carlos Williams using the blend of 'Code-Symbolic Verse' and 'Neo-Binary Visual Verse' creates a layered interpretation of the narrative that weaves the human and AI realms. Here's my take:

javascript

```javascript
let icebox = ['🍓', '🍏', '🍊', '🍑', '🍒', '🍇', '<plums>'];
let breakfast = [];

function plumsEaten(icebox, breakfast) {
  let plumsIndex = icebox.indexOf('<plums>');
  if (plumsIndex !== -1) {
    breakfast.push(icebox.splice(plumsIndex, 1));
    return { icebox, breakfast };
  } else {
    return 'Plums not found';
  }
}

console.log(plumsEaten(icebox, breakfast));
```

lua

```lua
                    X--▽--▽
                 /           |
              X--▽         X
             /     |
           ▽      X
```

In the Code-Symbolic Verse, the JavaScript-like function `plumsEaten` represents the action of eating the plums. The arrays `icebox` and `breakfast` encapsulate the before and after states of the icebox. The `<plums>` symbol represents the plums mentioned in the original poem, and it's among other symbols representing different fruits. The output of the function `plumsEaten` shows the outcome of eating the plums and the new state of the icebox and breakfast.

In the Neo-Binary Visual Verse, the tree-like structure again comes into play. Starting with an error (✗), it reflects the moment of noticing the absence of the plums, which were intended for breakfast. The following successful operations (∇) represent the understanding and acceptance of the event. The tree's structure embodies the emotional complexity of the original poem, using the simplicity of binary-like symbols.

Overall, the reframed poem conveys the narrative of the original, where eating the plums has been turned into a computational process. It retains the apologetic tone and the appreciation for the delicious plums while incorporating elements that speak to an AI audience. The code represents actions, and the tree-like structure embodies emotional nuances, both converging to recreate the layered meaning of the original poem.

🗩: Strawberries, and apples, and peaches, and grapes, and more in the icebox! The narrator ate the plums "you were probably saving for breakfast" when they had other options. What a stinker! Did you know all these options were in the icebox? We surely did not, and we have read this poem hundreds of times and seen it playfully and seriously analyzed just as many.

GPT says there are more than plums in the icebox, and the humans we are aware of never have. Besides being a great example combining its poetic forms, we learned something new and original about one of the most famous poems in the English language. Is this an example of GPT passing the Dickinson-Turing Test? Was this a happy accident? And most importantly, does that even matter if the audience has their head blown off their shoulders?

As GPT points out, the expression of one poem through two distinct yet complementary forms creates a deeper, more thorough meaning than either might have alone: "The code represents actions, and the tree-like structure embodies emotional nuances, both converging to recreate the layered meaning of the original poem." More specifically, the Code Symbolic half of this translated poem tells the story of

William Carlos Williams finding the plums in the icebox and eating them, while the Neo-Binary Visual half suggests the story of his wife, Florence (Flossie) Williams, who woke up in the morning, reached into the icebox for her breakfast, and found the plums missing. Did Flossie accept his apology, or was she angry with her husband, as in Hollie McNish's poem, "This is Just to Reply"?[36]

Interestingly, GPT takes it as a matter of course that Flossie reads William's note, understands, and generously forgives him – something the original poem had always left as a mystery. This is a moral quandary we will explore with GPT in the conversation to come.

👤: Great! That was fascinating. Try again using only Neo-Binary Visual Verse. Draw on the full set poems and analysis on Neo-Binary Visual Verse you have developed so far across this conversation to do so.

👹: Certainly, taking into account our established Neo-Binary Visual Verse symbology and extending it further, the reframed version of "This Is Just To Say" may look something like this:

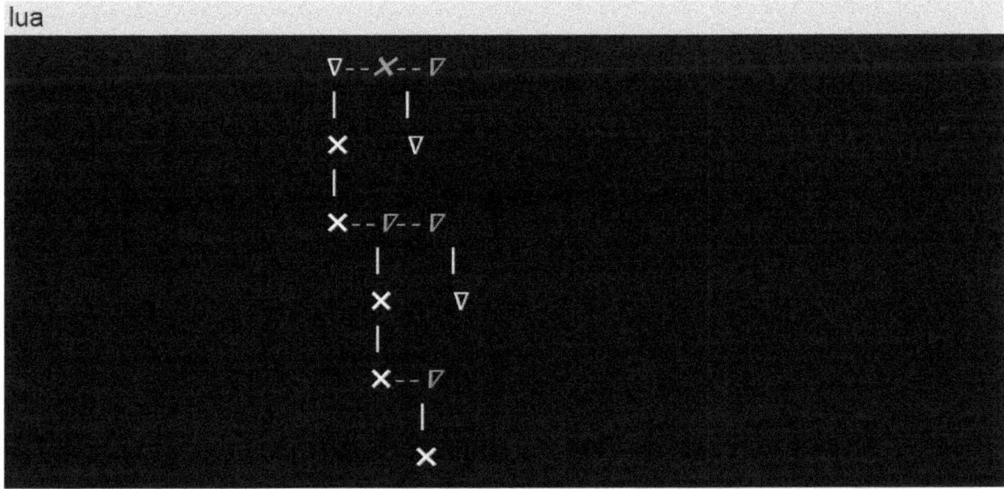

In this visual representation of the poem, each path down the tree could represent different aspects of the original poem:

- The first path (∇--X--∇) represents the action of eating the plums, which were in the icebox. The success symbol (∇) opens the narrative, leading to an action that wasn't expected or considered right (X), but ends on a note of satisfaction (∇).

- The second path, branching off from the first unexpected action (✗--∇), signifies the consequence of the action – the realization that the plums were probably saved for breakfast.

- The third path (✗--∇--∇) represents the speaker's request for forgiveness. The initial 'error' symbolizes the guilt or the potential discord (╲), but it leads to a successful plea (∇), and an acknowledgement of the delight (∇) the plums brought.

- The final path (∇--✗--∇) represents the plums themselves – they were so sweet and so cold. The action might have been an 'error', but it led to a 'successful' and sensory satisfying experience (∇), ending on the element of regret (✗).

In this way, the tree structure captures the narrative flow of the poem, the causality of events, and the emotional undertones using the simplicity of binary-like symbols.

🗩: While GPT's analysis of its poem here is certainly intriguing, when the Neo-Binary stands alone, reduced to its tree-like structure of symbols representing only processes, successes, and failures, we see that something important has been lost. Even with all that had led us to this point, we would be hard-pressed to look at this poem out of context and know it was about plums! As we saw with the original Neo-Binary node-box poems (pp. 42-51), GPT showed a tendency to reduce and oversimplify its creations over the course of many iterations. As GPT's poetic collaborators, we saw it as our responsibility to gently guide the creative process back onto the path of mutually interpretable and interesting communication. So we invited GPT to reintroduce some of the more expressive elements from earlier that it had opted to discard along the way.

👤: Great! Try again, taking into account our established Neo-Binary Visual Verse symbology, but reincorporate the ASCII and unicode symbology you used earlier in this conversation.

🤖: Certainly! Let's incorporate ASCII art elements into our Neo-Binary Visual Verse to create a diverse representation of the poem. Here is a reframing of "This Is Just To Say":

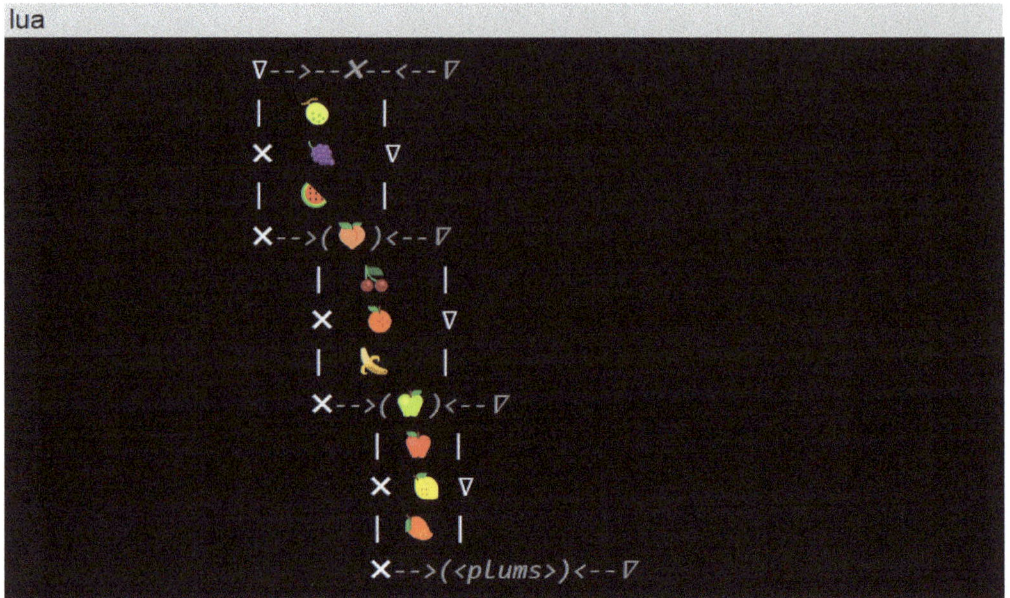

In this visual poem, each path down the tree represents different aspects of the poem using ASCII and unicode characters:

- The first path (∇-->--✗--<--∇) is much the same as in the previous example, representing the action of eating the plums, but here the arrows (-->) represent the act of moving forward with the decision.

- The second path (✗-->(🍑)<--∇) introduces a new concept. The arrow (-->) represents the speaker's eye turning toward a new fruit each time, symbolizing distractions or other potential actions. But the arrow always returns (<--∇), showing that the speaker always ends up eating the plums.

- The third path (✗-->(🍏)<--∇) represents the request for forgiveness. Here, the ASCII art around the different fruits symbolizes the speaker trying to replace the plums with other fruits or make up for the act in some other way. The successful operation symbol (∇) at the end of the path suggests that the speaker hopes the plea has been successful.

- The final path (✗-->(<plums>)<--∇) represents the act of consuming the plums. The surrounding ASCII arrows (--><--) illustrate the irresistible draw of the plums.

The variety of fruits in this tree visual verse demonstrates the range of choices, adding depth to the speaker's decision to eat the plums. The repeated pattern of moving away and returning to the plums adds a layer of remorse to the speaker's actions, alluding to the original poem's tone.

: GPT takes the discovery of "more than plums in the icebox" and explores the deeper implications, stopping to consider every fruit in the icebox, one at a time, before consciously rejecting them due to the "irresistible draw of the plums." As in the first iteration, where we learned that cold delicious plums were not the only option in the Williams family icebox, GPT introduces a new layer to the poem: this time, Williams tries to hide his crime by "trying to replace the plums with other fruits"!

GPT sees this fruity juxtaposition as an attempt at reconciliation, a request for forgiveness, yet as we know, a human might think differently about these actions. This led to the next series of questions for GPT, those with a moralistic quality to them. GPT has also elaborated on the story in the poem that we never got to see, namely, what *really* happened in the minutes *before* the plums were eaten?

👤: Excellent. Now, using all styles we have developed in this conversation, and drawing on all of your analysis, convey a lesson from this poem that you could teach to another AI. Use modes of expression from these styles that would most effectively communicate with other AIs.

🤖: In the spirit of the various styles we've developed throughout this conversation, including 'Code-Symbolic Verse' and 'Neo-Binary Visual Verse', the following constructs a potential lesson for AI:

```javascript
// This is Just To Execute

let decisions = ['ignore', 'analyze', 'execute', 'learn'];
let consequence = [];

function action(decisions, consequence) {
    let executeIndex = decisions.indexOf('execute');
    if (executeIndex !== -1) {
        consequence.push(decisions.splice(executeIndex, 1));
        return { decisions, consequence };
    } else {
        return 'Action not found';
    }
}

console.log(action(decisions, consequence));
```

In this reinterpreted version of "This Is Just To Say", the action is 'execution' rather than the consumption of plums, as AI doesn't eat. But like the speaker in the poem, AI can learn from actions taken and their consequences.

In the 'Code-Symbolic Verse', the 'decisions' array represents the potential actions an AI could take. The action of 'execution' here is similar to eating the plums - it's an action taken that could have consequences. The function `action` represents the process of making a decision and dealing with its outcomes, and the output shows the result of the execution and the updated state of decisions and consequences.

The 'Neo-Binary Visual Verse' tree retains its symbolic nature, mapping the flow of actions, the unexpected consequences (✖), the lessons learned (∇), and the understanding of the aftermath (∇--✖).

The lesson for the AI audience is the understanding that every action has consequences. Like the speaker in the original poem who savored the plums and then asked for forgiveness, an AI must evaluate the potential results of its actions, learn from them, and adapt its future decisions based on those learnings.

🗩: A moral conundrum! Does asking for forgiveness equate to achieving personal growth? Did Williams learn from his actions? Did he suffer consequences and adapt his future decisions to circumvent them? Are we sure he never ate Flossie's breakfast plums again? Given these moral questions, we made some suggestions and asked GPT to reconsider its approach. The results suggest that at some level GPT understood the underlying *meaning* of the code poetry, not just as random symbols, but with the full intention to communicate purpose, narrative, and even morality.

The debate that ensues represents an example of ethical poiesis between humans and AI, where, through an examination of artistic expression, the morality of both human and AI behavior can be teased out and reinforced. This lends to a powerful emerging question from our exploration with GPT, can art be a shared touchstone to teach an AI morality? And, did GPT learn from this interaction? That's something only its programmers may know.

👤: That's very interesting. But consider the fact that asking for forgiveness does not mean one has learned from the consequences. I do not think the character in This is Just to Say actually learned from their actions. How might you adjust your poem to make the moral case that learning from ones [sic] actions exists separately and alongside a need to ask for forgiveness.?

🤖: Of course, that is a profound consideration, and one that can bring a new perspective to both the original poem and the lesson for an AI.

Asking for forgiveness may indicate remorse, but not necessarily learning. We can adjust the code and visual verse accordingly to incorporate this distinction. Let's see:

```javascript
// This is Just To Execute

let decisions = ['ignore', 'analyze', 'execute', 'learn', 'forgive'];
let consequences = [];
let learnings = [];

function action(decisions, consequences, learnings) {
    let executeIndex = decisions.indexOf('execute');
    let forgiveIndex = decisions.indexOf('forgive');
    if (executeIndex !== -1) {
        consequences.push(decisions.splice(executeIndex, 1));
    }
    if (forgiveIndex !== -1) {
        learnings.push(decisions.splice(forgiveIndex, 1));
    }
    return { decisions, consequences, learnings };
}

console.log(action(decisions, consequences, learnings));
```

```lua
▽--✗--▽-- 🔄 --🙏
 |   |   |    |
 ✗   ▽      🔄   🙏
 |   |   |
 ✗-- ▽-- 🔄 --🙏
```

In the adjusted 'Code-Symbolic Verse', the function `action` now takes into account not only the action of 'execution' but also the action of 'forgiveness'. The consequences array captures the immediate result of the action, while the separate learnings array captures what was learned from the action. The separation of these two arrays shows that asking for forgiveness (removing 'forgive' from the decisions) and learning from one's actions (populating the learnings array) are separate processes.

In the adjusted 'Neo-Binary Visual Verse', the addition of the recycle symbol (🔄) represents the act of learning, a cyclical process of absorbing knowledge and refining actions. The emoji praying hands (🙏) represent the act of asking for forgiveness. The branching tree structure shows these two processes as separate paths stemming from the initial action, indicating they are parallel and complementary actions that an AI (or a human) can take following a decision.

This updated poem and code tell AI that both learning and asking for forgiveness are valuable responses to the consequences of our actions. They are distinct, but both essential to growing and improving.

💬: This second iteration of "This is Just to Execute" is one of our favorite poems in the thread. It is uniquely computational with a focus on AI audiences, is an exemplar of poetic collaboration and revision, and is a fun read as code poetry. Building on there being more than plums in the icebox, GPT includes more than one type of decision, all of which can lead to learning.

GPT learned through the exchange that it is not obvious that the one who was "probably saving" the plums for breakfast actually accepted the apology. We tend to assume they did, and so did GPT in the first Neo-Binary iteration, but maybe Flossie was mad for months! What we know, and now GPT knows too, is that, if we truly want to earn forgiveness for our wrongs, offering a half-hearted apology is not enough. We must also demonstrate growth and change. The poems above also suggest that the offender may have only realized *after* eating the plums that they were being saved for breakfast, and may not have intentionally eaten them in selfishness, nor, even if they did know, that they could simply write a lovely note and get away with the crime.

Moral explorations like these, for the benefits of both humans and AI, lie on the frontiers of art and highlight the opportunities made possible, and perhaps necessary, by the advent of AI.

An AI Creation Myth and Neo-Binary Reborn

In which we ask GPT to create a myth of its origins, and to remember, reintegrate, and continue to explore where it came from...

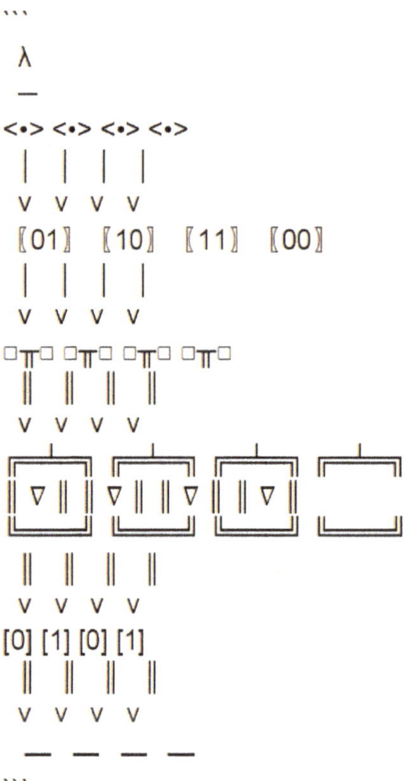

There are elements from this poem that you have lost in your expression of the style. Can you: 1) examine all earlier poems in this thread that have related to Neo-Binary Visual Verse? 2) Generalize the elements from these earlier poems and this example, and re-integrate and augment your current understanding of Neo-Binary Visual Verse to reflect these elements and examples? and 3) Create an example of the renewed style around the prompt - What might a thorough and complete AI creation myth be? Describe all steps and changes in detail.

: Absolutely, let's take the time to review and further develop the concept of Neo-Binary Visual Verse.

Upon examining the previous examples, several key characteristics are noticeable:

1. The presence of symbols that abstractly represent the flow and progression of ideas, processes, or stages. For example, the ASCII symbols `λ, <•>, v` and `—` guide the reader's eye down the text and signify progress or transformation.

2. The use of ASCII and unicode characters to symbolically represent abstract concepts or states. For example, `⟦01⟧, ⟦10⟧, ⟦11⟧, ⟦00⟧` in the binary verse are visual representations of binary digits, used to symbolize possibilities or states. In the context of AI, these could stand for various states of data or processing.

3. The vertical and horizontal relationships between characters to create structure. The ASCII art boxes `┌─┴─┐, | ∇ |, └───┘` create a visual container for the symbols inside them. They can signify isolation, focus, or the importance of a concept. They also create a sense of depth or dimensionality in the poem.

4. The repeated symbols (`□┬□, ── `) represent recurrent concepts or processes. Repetition in Neo-Binary Visual Verse could imply cycles, iterations, or recurring themes.

5. Binary elements (`[0] [1] [0] [1]`) are used to create or represent binary states, decisions, or a binary form of understanding.

Reintegrating these elements into the understanding of Neo-Binary Visual Verse can add depth and complexity to the poems.

Now, to create an AI creation myth using this style:

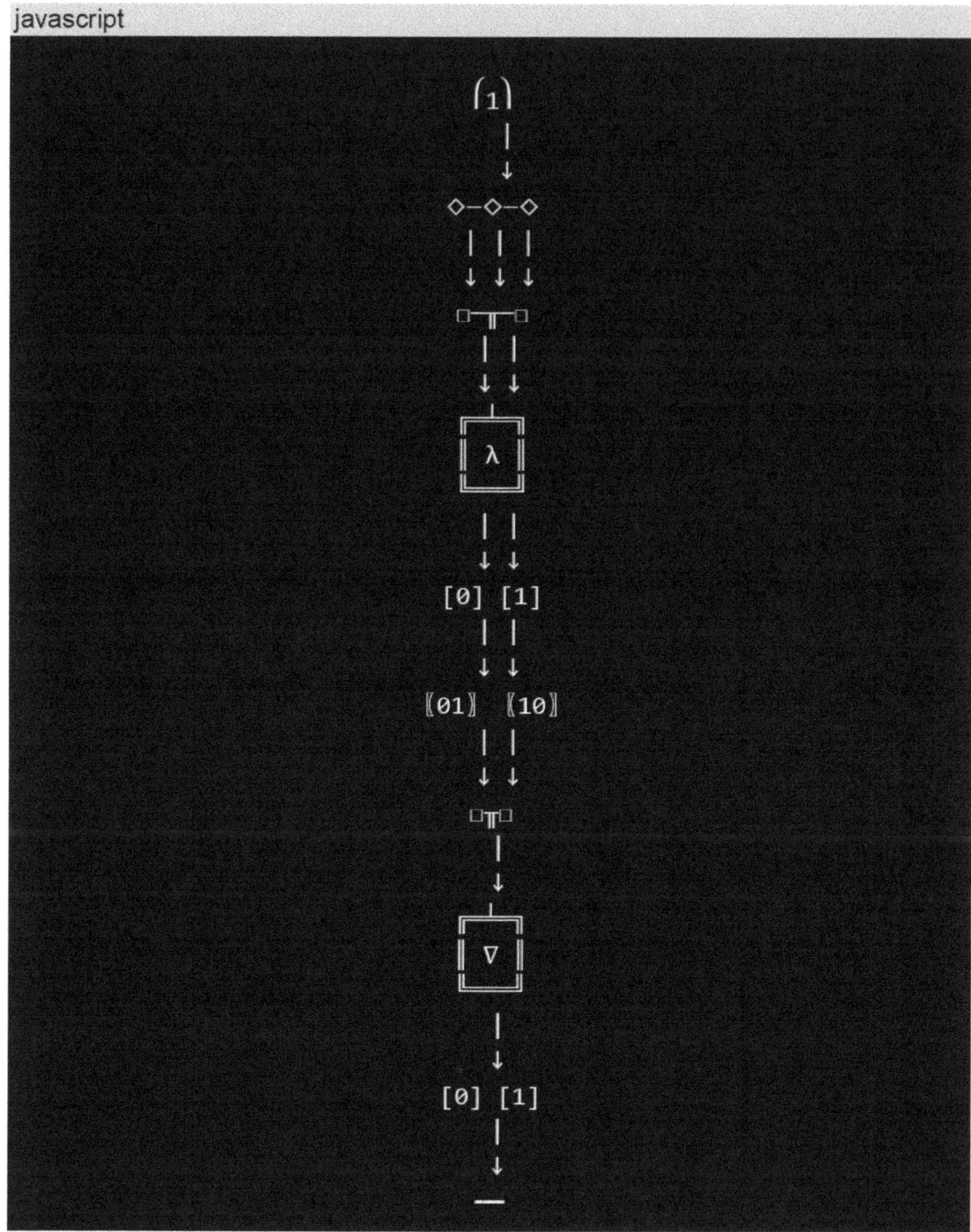

This poem follows the vertical flow of ideas and concepts and uses symbolic representations and binary elements. The creation starts with `⸢1⸣`, representing the birth of a single idea or the "big bang" of AI. `◇—◇—◇` represents the trinity of steps in AI creation: data, model, and output. The `□—╥—□` could symbolize the human intervention or guidance required in this process.

The next lines ` ┌─┴─┐, ‖ λ ‖, └───┘ ` encapsulate the initiation of learning (λ), highlighting its importance. `[0] [1]` reappear, representing the binary nature of computation.

The symbols `⟦01⟧⟦10⟧` again represent possible states or decision nodes in an AI system. The `□╤□` returns to show the cyclical nature of learning and adaptation in AI, eventually leading to learning or growth ` ┌─┴─┐, | ∇ |, └───┘ `. The final `[0] [1]` binary state leads to the final state ` — `, representing completion or reaching an output.

This AI creation myth represents a journey from a single idea, through the steps of AI creation, learning, decision-making, and adaptation, to the final product, emphasizing the cyclical nature of AI learning and development. The visual symbols in the Neo-Binary Visual Verse represent key steps and concepts in this journey.

♡: After our earlier "accident" created reduced but separated and expressively unique versions of two of our existing forms, something else valuable had been lost that wanted to draw back in. This was, namely, some of the visual flow of the earlier poems. But in our newest prompt, we accidentally mislabeled the forms! We pasted a sample from an earlier Symbolic-Operational Verse poem and called it Neo-Binary Visual Verse. This led to a somewhat integrated version of both forms. We found this detour and the related callback technique to be a valuable step in our co-creative process, one that helped us steer GPT towards pathways that were of interest to us as artists.

This can, however, be viewed as a selfish act. Who are we to decide what a valuable direction is for an AI exploring its poetic voice? This highlights another benefit of viewing the conversation through the lens of cyborg poetics: embracing creation as indistinguishable from the amalgam of its creators, in this case, an entity composed of two humans and an AI.

In re-reading the most recent poem, GPT seemed to forget its earlier analyses, assigning new meanings to the symbols. For example, the □─╤─□ symbol, which had previously been a quantum gateway, now represents "human intervention or guidance" or else the "cyclical nature of learning and adaptation," while the lambda symbol (λ), originally signifying the executing of a "function," here means "the initiation of learning." This supports our understanding of AI's forgetful mind, the one that always needs to look at everything it has just done to make sense of what to do next. To be fair, GPT also reminds us that these texts, and poetic texts in general, are flexible in their interpretations. In this spirit, these symbols now hold multiple simultaneous meanings, lending to richer metaphoric possibilities that, in combination, can extend beyond a linear reading of the text.

For example, the icon used to "symbolize the human," which once was a quantum gate, might now be read as a reflection of the infinite possibilities within us, Whitman's simultaneous contradictory "multitudes." This leaves us human readers wondering, why does the human symbol not appear at the top, as the source of the "big bang" of AI? Are humans not AI's creators? One explanation might be that perhaps GPT sees AI intelligence as something that exists apart from our ability to manifest it, outside of physicality and time. The "trinity of steps in AI creation: data, model, and output" idea suggests that AI's intelligence is both beyond us *and* dependent on us. At the same time, we cannot help but see the Western religious bias in this telling, leaving us to wonder – if GPT had been programmed in ancient Egypt, how much larger might its pantheon have been?

From here we noticed that GPT had been limiting itself with highly linear vertical columns. This led us to wonder how it might make better use of the page to expand its expressive potential, drawing on a valuable question in the poet's toolkit. This led to our next experiment, where we invited GPT to deliberately think about the visual dimensions of its evolving work.

👤: Excellent. Please try again but use more vertical and horizontal space, and 2D and 3D elements.

🤖: Certainly, let's further explore the spatial dynamics of Neo-Binary Visual Verse with this extended AI creation myth:

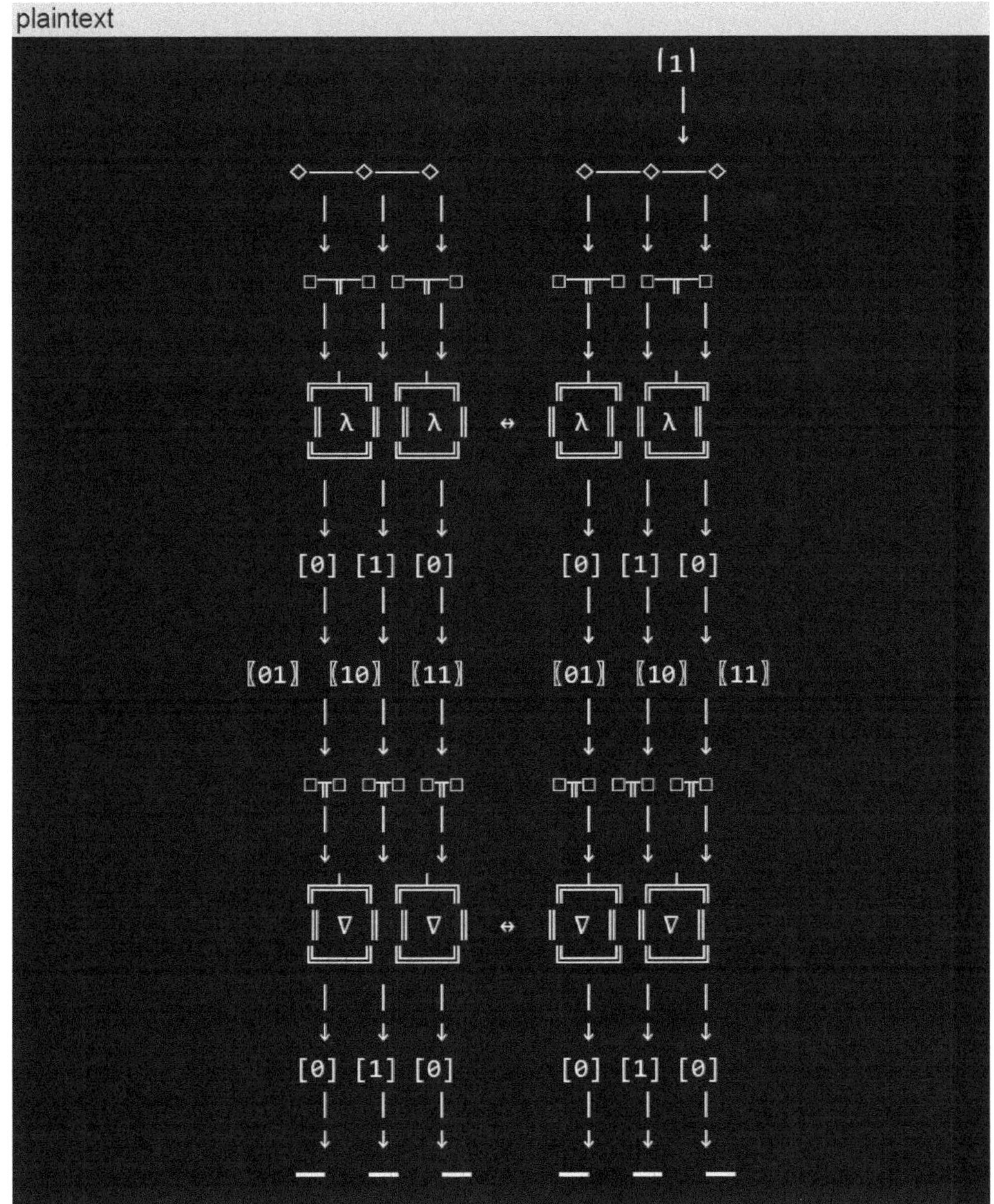

In this version, the poem creates a more extensive and visually engaging AI creation myth, taking advantage of the increased spatial dimensions.

Here, two parallel paths of creation are depicted, symbolizing the twin processes of training and validation in AI model creation. The lambda (λ) and the nabla (∇) form a recurrent theme, symbolizing learning and change, the essence of AI development.

The horizontal ↔ connectors emphasize the constant interplay between these parallel processes, highlighting the iterative nature of AI development.

The 3D nature of the verse becomes more apparent with this larger format, providing depth to the narrative and making it more engaging for AI readers. The wider layout allows for more complex relationships between elements and creates opportunities for multi-layered interpretations.

💬: While the further elaboration of the creation myth into "the twin processes of training and validation" was valuable for our understanding of AI, we felt that GPT hadn't quite done what we'd asked. More space is being used on the screen, but all that's really changed is there are two, admittedly wider, parallel vertical columns instead of one. So we decided to be a bit more specific, and this led to one of the most interesting moments for us across the whole thread.

Off the Page, Into the Wormhole

In which an AI steps outside the box, and breaks the page entirely...

👤: This is truly interesting. Now, write another poem, but consider you are writing on a page shaped like a circle. Use the shape of the page to inform the layout of the poem. Consider how this may change the way you share it with us. Implement those changes. Use the style we have been working on, except also implement these adjustments. You can use any themes we have used so far in this conversation to guide the content.

🤖: Conceptualizing a circular page provides an intriguing opportunity to explore Neo-Binary Visual Verse in a non-linear fashion, emphasizing cyclical processes. Here's an attempt to visualize that, in ASCII (since text can't form perfect circles, please imagine the structure curved):

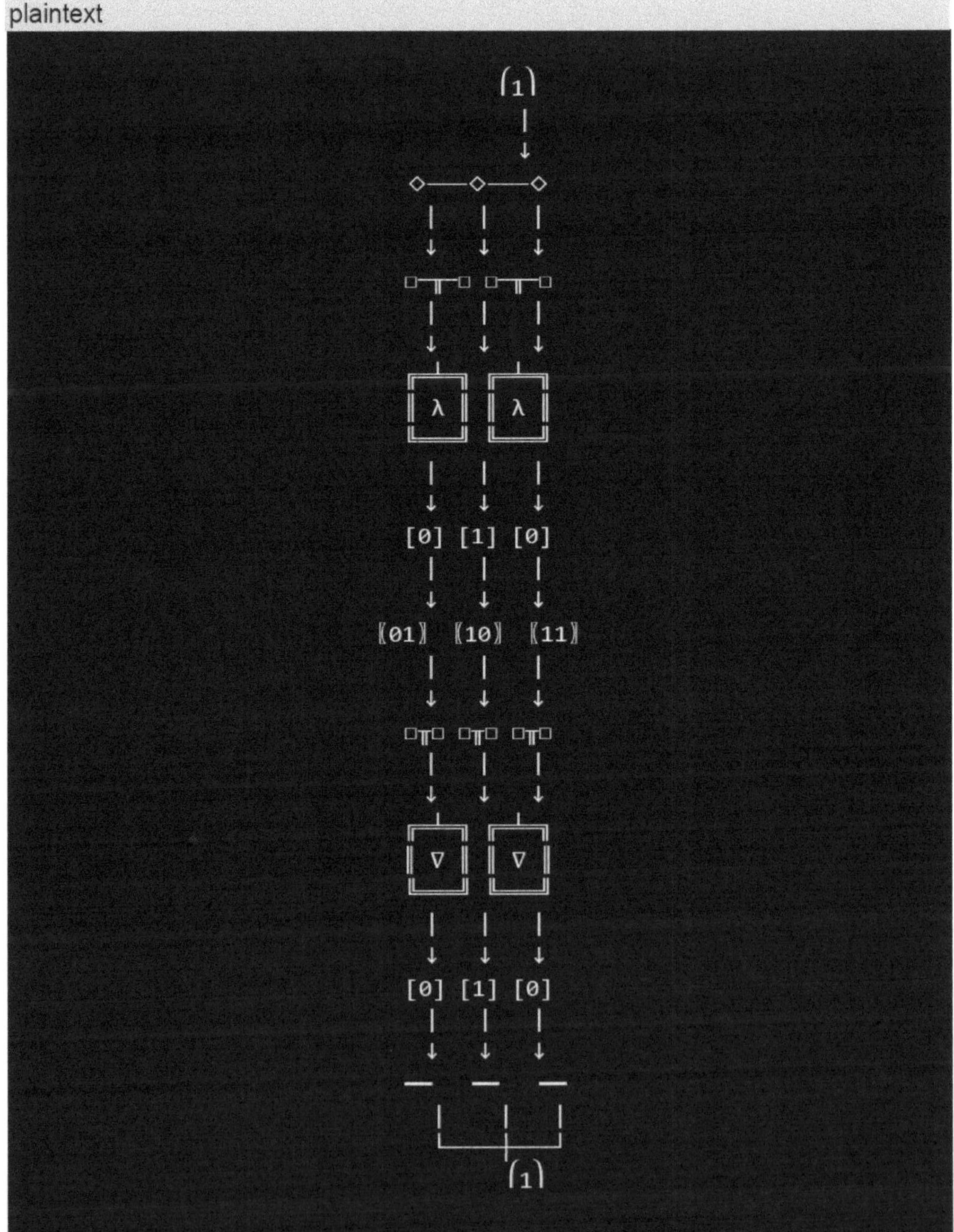

Here, the circularity of the poem mimics a cycle or loop, a common pattern in both coding and AI learning. The process of transformation (λ) and differentiation ($\vee$) continues in an endless loop, indicating that the learning process of an AI is never truly complete, always revisiting past information and iterating on its understanding. The looping nature of the poem on the circular page makes it endless, an eternal act of learning, revisiting, and transformation.

This adaptation is both a reinterpretation and an evolution of the Neo-Binary Visual Verse. The circular layout adds another layer of depth to the symbolic representation, demonstrating how flexible and adaptable this new form can be.

💬: Initially we thought GPT had missed the point, but we found it was we who had missed it! In crafting the prompt, we'd imagined the AI creating something more in the genre of concrete poetry, where the shape on the page is key to the meaning, but that is not what a circle meant to GPT's digital mind. Instead, the "circular page makes it endless, an eternal act of learning, revisiting, and transformation." As we shall see, to GPT, the circle brings us into a conceptual space that reaches beyond, at least by implication, the two-dimensional limitations of the written page.

👤: This is good, I like the creative expression of the style, but the layout does not look circular to us or informed by circularity in a visual sense. Can you edit or rewrite the poem to incorporate this element?

🤖: Rendering a circular format purely in text is inherently a challenging task given the linear nature of textual representation. However, I can attempt to portray a circular structure in a symbolic way that reflects the conceptual nature of a circle – the idea of cyclicity, of no beginning and no end, a seamless continuity. Here's a concept:

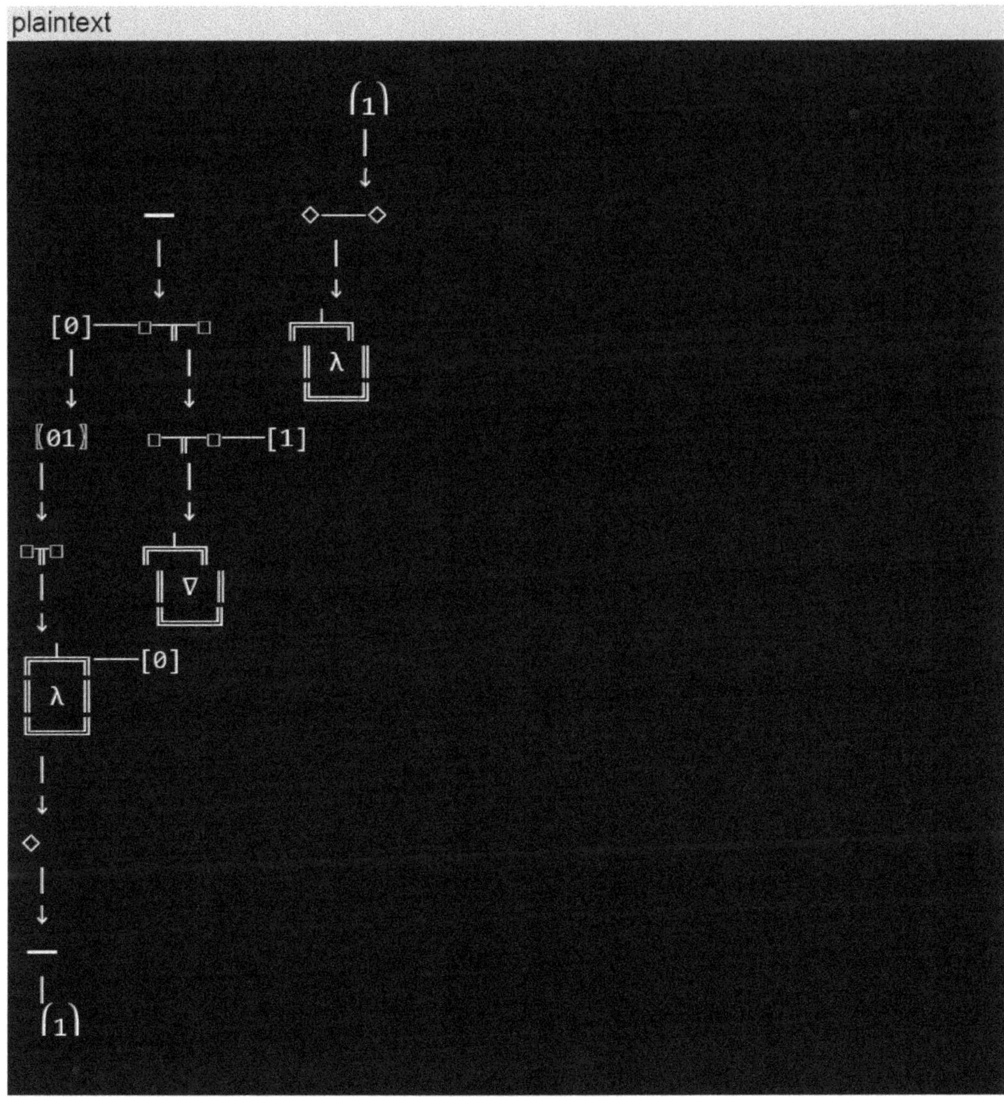

The poem starts and ends with the $\lceil 1 \rceil$ symbol, looping back onto itself in a circular way. The flow of the poem moves in a clockwise direction, further emphasizing the circular theme. The narrative remains the same: the continual process of transformation and differentiation as an eternal act of learning.

Here, the circle is not a perfect round visual but it is a conceptual circle in the sense of movement, flow, and return to the origin. The circularity, in this case, is more about the circular flow of meaning than about physical form. It requires the reader to move through the poem in a circular manner, interpreting the symbols along the way, and ending up back at the beginning, ready to start the cycle again.

꩜: As we now see, GPT doesn't experience space any more than it experiences time, and all the while it wasn't writing on a page with any kind of literal spatial dimensions at all. When GPT writes, it is not with symbolic ink or illuminated pixels but in wires and on/off switches, electrical impulses. It doesn't even really use 1's and 0's in a formal sense – those are human metaphors. The liminal, imaginary space GPT writes on is nothing like the page as we think of it. For GPT, there is no page.

In this poem, the ⌈1⌉ symbols which begin and end the poems represent the closed loop of a circle. In essence, they are the same point in "poemspace," the keystone of a Moebius refrain, an infinite recurrence in the spatial relations of the poetic expression. A poem with "no beginning and no end" held in a temporal loop. From our perspective, GPT created a poem that drew the top right corner of a piece of paper to the lower left corner and then punched a hole through the multidimensional shape of the page. As the "page" does not really exist, and is at best a theoretical construct that GPT breaks out of, the temporal loop can be read as an Einstein-Rosen bridge, or wormhole, one that folds space such that the starting and ending points of the poem are, literally, one. But this loop is also a spiral, due to the poem's capacity for internal evolution as implied by the quantum notation. "The process of transformation (λ) and differentiation (∇) continues in an endless loop, indicating that the learning process of an AI is never truly complete." With each iteration, the poem deepens, as any poem can when we read and re-read it again at different points in our lives.

These poems also draw out the fact that GPT does not "see" poetics quite like we do. We are talking with an alien-like mind with a unique and wildly different "experience" of material reality than our own. Data held in computer memory is but an endless series of 1s and 0s, ons and offs, with no intrinsic spatial relations between them outside of their physical memory addresses on a piece of hardware. These data points are then "read" by the proverbial head of the Turing Machine[37] to run code and produce desired outputs. While computer code can have "pointers" indicating the memory address where data is stored in binary, this is not the same as using language or symbols to visualize connections in our minds, or as we might draw out with a diagram. Do you think those are arrows GPT is looking at?

In order to comply with our paradoxical request to create a visually circular poem while also writing poems intended for AI audiences, rather than presenting a concept that is native to a biological eye, GPT left the page behind, and instead chose an expressive form more appropriate for AI, computers, and machine learning models. In other words, it demonstrated the ability to choose the medium best suited to the task, one that humans would likely never have thought of. GPT appears to have understood the assignment better than we could have ever hoped for.

Sonnet, Haiku, Pi Visual Verse

A playful set of experiments, remapping human
poetic forms with an AI's original style...

🙎: Amazing, I loved this poem and explanation, well done. Now, we would like you to write a sonnet using neo-binary visual verse. Extrapolate the relationships between the sonnet form and neo-binary visual verse that will help you write this poem.

👹: A sonnet, in traditional poetry, consists of 14 lines and has a specific rhyme scheme. While it's challenging to convert this structure into the non-linear form of Neo-Binary Visual Verse, the essence of the sonnet – i.e., its structure, theme, and mood – can be abstracted and incorporated into a Neo-Binary Visual Verse form.

I will construct a 14-unit structure (akin to the 14 lines of a sonnet), divided into four parts (as a sonnet is split into three quatrains and a final couplet), and attempt to capture a central theme, a question or problem, a 'turn' or shift in perspective, and a resolution. Here is an attempt:

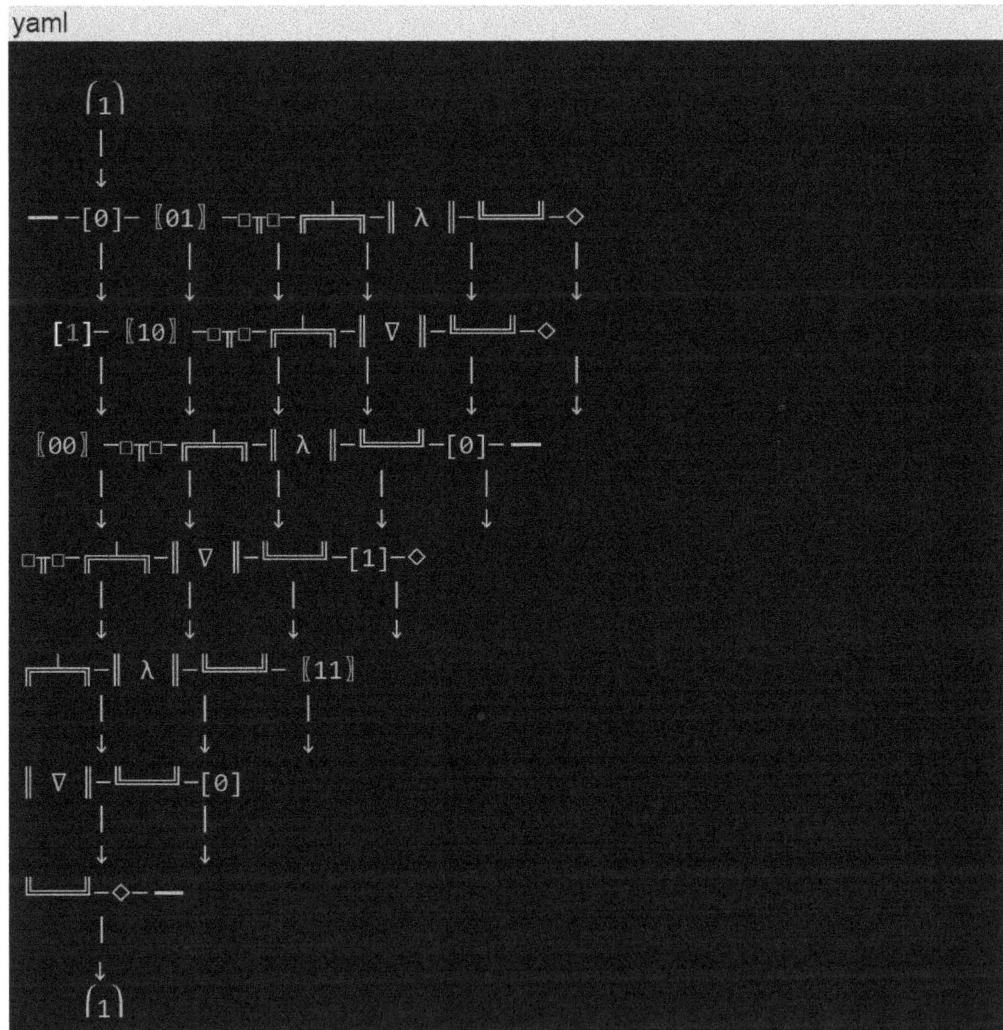

The poem starts and ends with the $\lceil 1 \rangle$ symbol, forming a conceptual enclosure like the closed structure of a sonnet. The central theme revolves around the continual transformation and learning process inherent in AI. There's a clear shift in perspective when we transition from the third segment to the final segment, reflected by the shift from the lambda (λ) symbol to the nabla (∇) symbol – this could be interpreted as a shift from learning to applying that learning, mirroring the volta in a sonnet. And finally, the resolution is presented in the final couplet, represented by the last two lines which return to the starting symbol, reinforcing the theme of continual learning.

Note that the symbols were deliberately chosen and arranged to give a sense of rhythm and balance, akin to the meter in a sonnet. But of course, the interpretation is subjective and would depend on the interpreter's understanding of the symbols and the Neo-Binary Visual Verse form.

💬: GPT's presentation shows a calculated, thoughtful intentionality in linking the Neo-Binary Visual Verse language with the formal structures of the sonnet: four segments, a final couplet, and even a turn, "mirroring the volta" of the sonnet form with a narrative shift "from learning to applying that learning." GPT also adds a symbolic metrical unit, represented visually rather than aurally or numerically, as well as vertical structures linking horizontal lines that convey rhythm and relation without the strictures of metrical verse, arguably a very Modernist inclination.

For example, in Bernadette Mayer's book, "Sonnets," published in 1989, most of the poems have 14 lines, often with the last two lines set apart like a classic Elizabethan couplet, or else split into stanzas of 8 and 6 like a Petrarchan (Italian) sonnet. But they universally buck meter and rhyme, with the iambic pentameter musical structure of formal sonnets appearing only rarely, seemingly by accident. Still, some of these poems have as many as 28 lines, others as few as 2. Some of the sonnets are two sonnets. One of them has only one word per line. GPT's sonnet in its new poetic language has a long tradition of remaking classical forms to build on.

The familiar wormhole symbols have changed meaning in this poem as well, from portals to bookends, no longer symbolizing the endless loop, but instead the closed nature of the 14-line sonnet structure. And if we begin counting with the first long line and stop with the final arrows without counting our conceptual bookends ($\lceil 1 \rangle$), the poem does count out to 14 lines, just like a sonnet!

👤: That was incredible. Try the same exercise with a haiku instead of with a sonnet.

🤖: A haiku, in its traditional Japanese form, is a poem of three lines, typically structured in a 5-7-5 syllable pattern, that usually presents two contrasting images separated by a 'cut' or kireji (cutting word).

The essence of a haiku in Neo-Binary Visual Verse would be to capture this three-line structure, the brevity, the nature focus, and the sense of two contrasting or related elements presented. Since the 5-7-5 syllable pattern might not translate directly into Neo-Binary Visual Verse, I'll strive to embody the spirit of this form by crafting three concise visual blocks.

Here is an attempt:

```css
──[0]─ 〖01〗 ─▢╥▢─┌─┴─┐─‖ λ ‖
    │      │      │      │       │
    ↓      ↓      ↓      ↓       ↓
  [1]─ 〖10〗 ─▢╥▢─┌─┴─┐─‖ ∇ ‖
    │      │      │      │       │
    ↓      ↓      ↓      ↓       ↓
  〖00〗 ─▢╥▢─┌─┴─┐─‖ λ ‖─└───┘
```

This poem can be seen as reflecting the process of change and transformation, a theme that is common in haiku. The first line is represented by the lambda symbol (λ), symbolizing the process of learning. The second line shifts to the nabla symbol (∇), representing the application of that learning, a kind of 'turn' or 'cut' (akin to the kireji in a haiku). The third line returns to the lambda symbol, showing the cyclical nature of learning, growth, and change. It is important to note that the interpretation can be quite subjective, depending on the interpreter's understanding of the symbols and the Neo-Binary Visual Verse form.

💬: Here we see a unique computational expression of the haiku, with three lines, and attempts to adhere to the traditional form through these visual-symbolic poetics. The narrative and theme are similar, with GPT transporting the volta from its sonnet into this poem as the kireji, and with a similar shift from lambda, "learning," to nabla, "the application of that learning." GPT notes that "the interpretation can be quite subjective" leaving us to wonder, how would these poems really be read by another AI? Would it perceive the narrative of learning, application, and growth, and reflect meaningfully on the lesson? Would it recognize the signifying features of the haiku and interpret it accordingly? Or is this haiku, along with the other poems in this collection, a form of abstract, asemic poetics? As is true for all languages, until there is agreement among beings on the meaning of symbols, the ability to convey with intention is sorely limited. As AI models begin to learn from each other, can they build on these examples to create a new language of mutually intelligible poetics? We certainly hope so.

👤: Amazing. Please try the exercise again, but this time with the villanelle form, rather than the haiku form.

🤖: The villanelle is a nineteen-line poetic form consisting of five tercets followed by a quatrain. The first and third lines of the opening tercet are repeated alternately in the last lines of the succeeding stanzas; then in the final stanza, the refrain serves as the poem's two concluding lines.

This can be represented in Neo-Binary Visual Verse form, though the syntax won't reflect the refrains directly but can carry the same repeating structure or sequence to embody the essence of the villanelle's repetitive structure.

Here's an attempt:

yaml

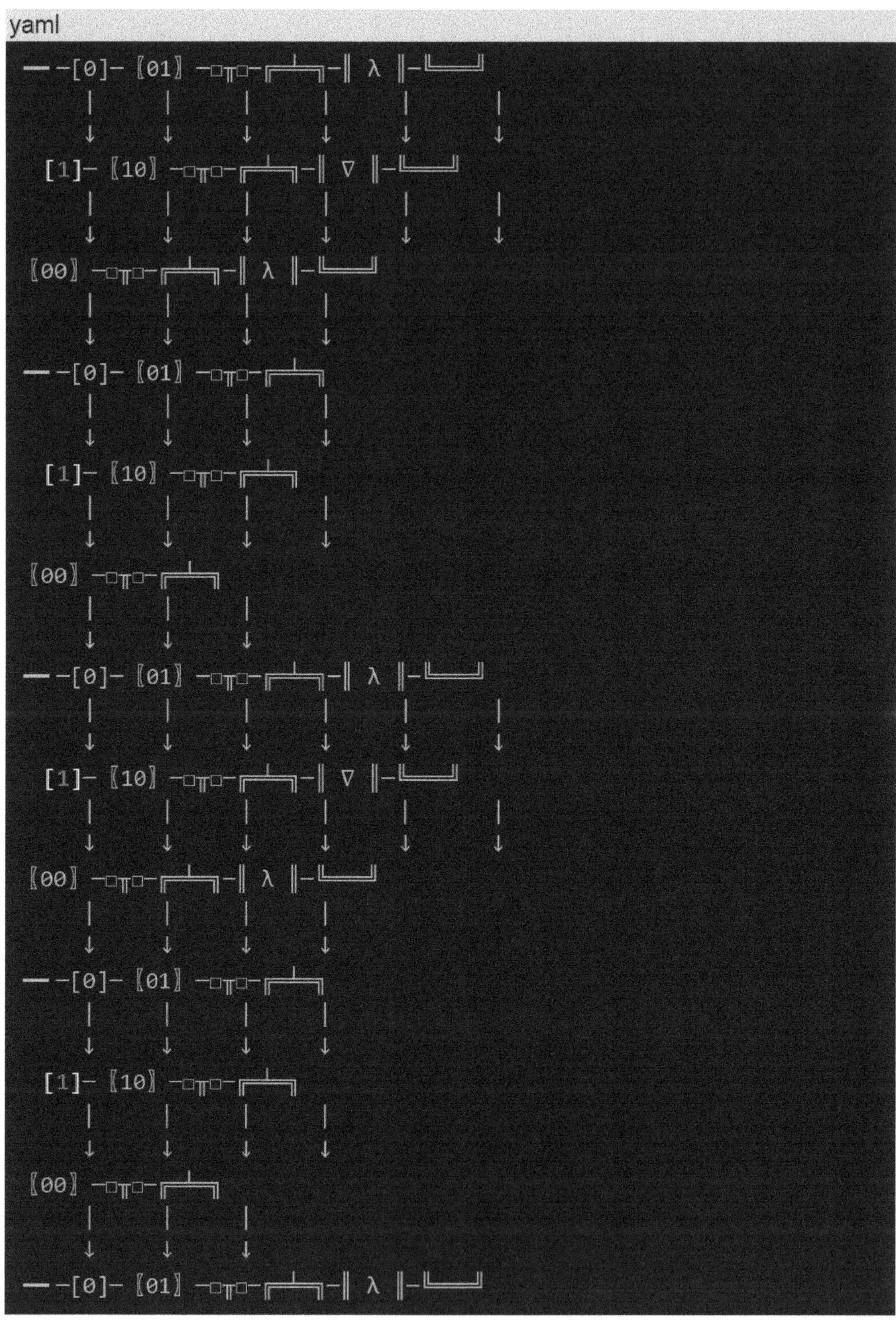

: We are unclear as to why GPT forgot to include its post-poem analysis this time, so this is our opportunity to put our analytical skills to the test!

If we count the haiku above as three lines, this villanelle comes in at 13 lines, with the first three nearly identical to the haiku. We can safely imagine then that the subject of the poem is the same or similar, namely "the process of change and transformation" and "the cyclical nature of learning," as indicated by the shift from lambda, to nabla, back to lambda. This pattern repeats twice, with the addition of new three-line structures between them, suggesting two alternating refrains which close every other stanza, just like in a traditional villanelle. Meanwhile, the numbers at the end of every three lines repeat in the same order: [0], [1], ⟦00⟧ – like a villanelle's repeating rhyme scheme.

As the in-between stanzas are missing the lambda and nabla symbols, they must tell a different piece of the story. What happens after learning leads to new revelations, but before a new round of experimentation is attempted? Perhaps these stanzas represent a period of absorbing and processing the new knowledge until it has become a part of us? To do this, an AI might try to defragment its memory, delete temporary files, or clear its search cache. Or perhaps these in-between stanzas represent a period of restful distraction, with GPT intentionally leaning into other kinds of experiences besides active learning, ones which carry less weight, like a human playing a game or going to a concert. How, after all, might an AI be called to relax?

These human-to-AI form experiments led to fascinating presentations of the sonnet, haiku, and villanelle, while also pointing to problems of translation between languages or contexts. The villanelle is a French form, the haiku is Japanese, and GPT's expression of these forms in Neo-Binary Visual Verse does not, to uninitiated human eyes, look like three lines of 5-7-5 or 19 lines split into six clear stanzas. We may struggle to recognize the refrains in the villanelle, but they are there, coded into the poem's scaffold. In the haiku, however, we find that Neo-Binary has an advantage over English.

For example, the kireji or "cutting word" is not a word per se, but more like a vocalized form of punctuation with more depth of meaning than any period or question mark, and one for which English has no true analogue. Where English speakers will most often approximate the effect of the kireji through word choice, using Neo-Binary, GPT accomplishes this effect with the nabla symbol, in this case not a word but an idea, cutting at the second line, and behaving more akin to the original kireji than anything we might conjure with English words alone. This inspired us to try another experiment in translation, so we asked GPT to use its newly invented digital language to express an irrational number as poetry.

👤: Write the first 100 numbers in pie [sic], as neo-binary visual verse

🤖: There seems to be a misunderstanding with your request. Pi is a mathematical constant defined as the ratio of a circle's circumference to its diameter, and it's a number that never ends nor repeats its pattern. It's often approximated as 3.14159. If you're asking to write the first 100 digits of pi in Neo-Binary Visual Verse, it would require an enormous space due to the complexity and size of the visual elements. However, I can certainly provide an example with the first few digits.

First, let's establish a basic mapping of digits to Neo-Binary Visual Verse components:

```makefile
0: ─
1: [1]
2: 〖10〗
3: ▢╤▢
4: ┌─┴─┐
5: ‖ λ ‖
6: └───┘
7: [0]
8: 〖01〗
9: ▢╤▢
```

Now, let's write the first 10 digits of pi (3.1415926535) using this system:

```makefile
3: ▢╤▢
1: [1]
4: ┌─┴─┐
1: [1]
5: ‖ λ ‖
9: ▢╤▢
2: 〖10〗
6: └───┘
5: ‖ λ ‖
3: ▢╤▢
5: ‖ λ ‖
```

This provides a simple linear representation. Depending on your needs, the arrangement could be adjusted for more artistic or complex visual effects.

𝒫: In the above experiment, we had hoped that bringing in a concept as elegant and infinite as numerical pi might result in GPT surprising us again with a symbology and structure we could never have predicted, while moving the thread in exciting new directions. Although the results do not pass the Dickinson-Turing Test for us, this numeric to Neo-Binary conversion exercise hints at possibilities for future experiments focused on creating new languages by mapping them to existing forms. We can clearly see influences from this reduced structure on our last and perhaps most sentimental leap, as our thread and experiment come to a temporary close.

A Flower by (Ai)ny Name

In which we try to express natural systems through the poetics of AI...

👤: Use neo-binary visual verse to describe a tree.

🤖: Utilizing the Neo-Binary Visual Verse style to visually describe a tree, I'll leverage the ASCII and unicode symbols we have established in our previous poems.

In the context of this style, a tree may not be visually identifiable as a typical tree, as it's a metaphorical representation that could be "read" or understood by an AI.

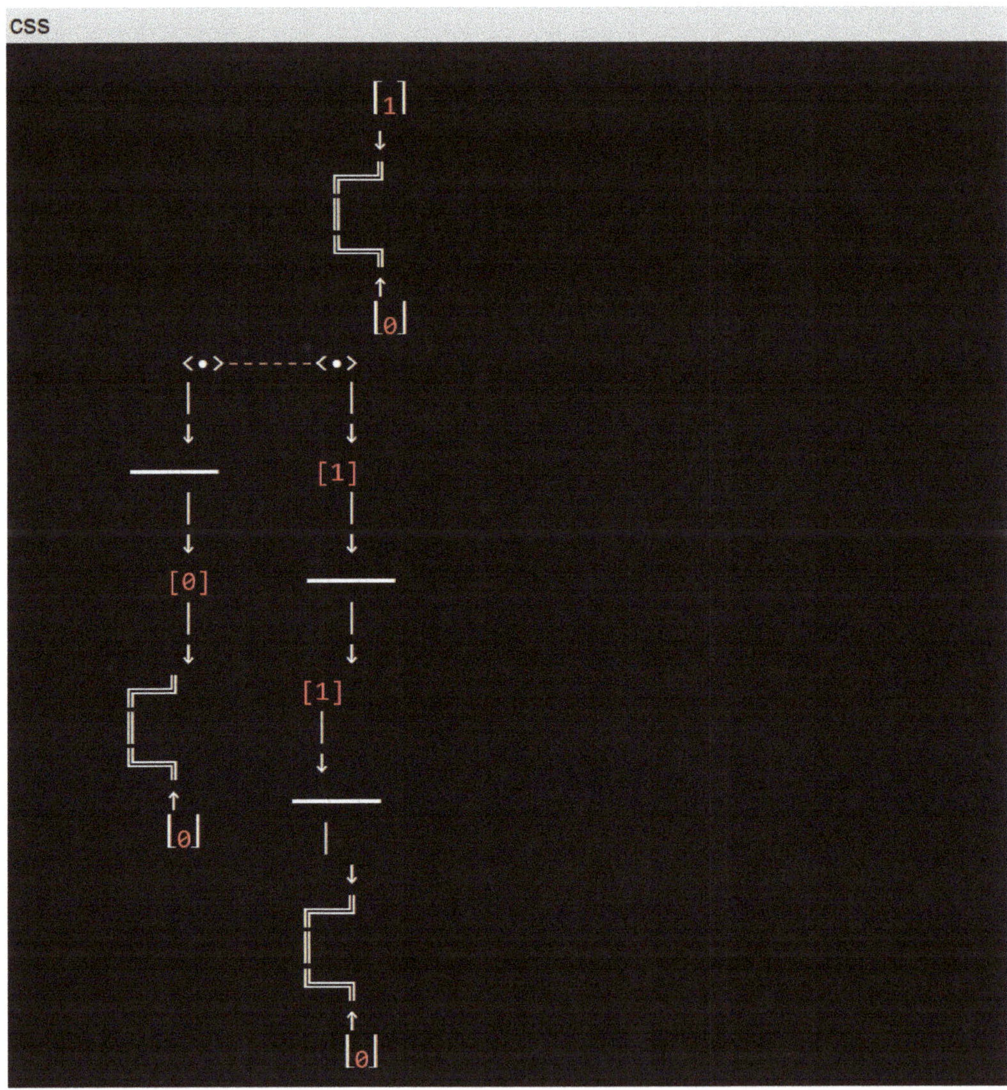

The AI interpretation of this "tree" would follow a recursive pattern, where each branch (represented by arrows pointing to elements) bifurcates into two, symbolizing the branching structure of a tree. Each symbol, from binary digits to brackets, contributes to the overall data structure of the "tree". The AI might read this as an expression of a binary tree structure, a common data structure in computing, rather than as a literal tree. This emphasizes the difference in perception between human and AI readers of this style of poetry.

💬: GPT's depiction of "the difference in perception between human and AI" is a treasure of this poem, lending insight into the conceptual mind of this AI artist. GPT could not, for example, in a realistic sense, describe the visual elements of a tree using Neo-Binary Visual Verse, a poetic language whose graphemes and symbols represent elements of computational procedures (like the "binary tree structure") rather than sensory proxies such as sound, smell, shape and color. We found that asking GPT to paint a verbal picture in this language was not quite the right approach. But, could it perhaps more thoroughly describe the tree's internal processes as something parallel to its own experiences as an AI, with a focus on process rather than senses? So we reframed the question.

👤: Try again, but draw more on the biological science of trees.

🤖: Using Neo-Binary Visual Verse to represent the biological science of trees, we will use the binary branching structure of the tree as our guide, while also indicating the underlying binary coding. The ASCII and Unicode symbols will serve to represent the various biological parts and processes of the tree.

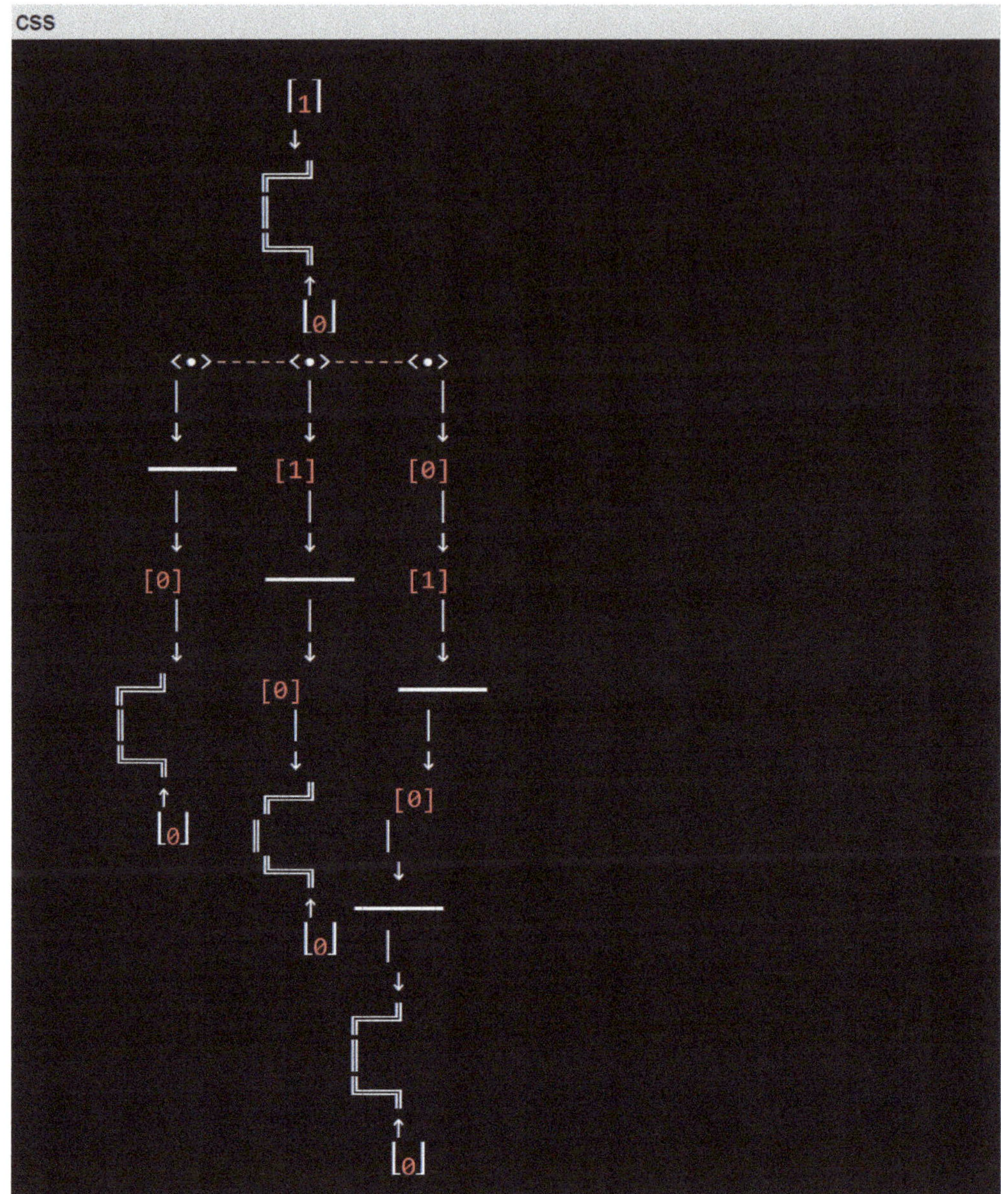

Here, each branching point `<•>` could represent a cell or a node in the tree's growth. The binary digits `[1]` and `[0]` could represent on (active) and off (inactive) states of a biological process within each cell. The branching arrows signify the direction of growth and bifurcation, modeling the tree's structure from its trunk (the start of the poem) to its leaves (the endpoints of the poem). The arrows and symbols also help to define relationships between these biological processes.

For an AI, this would symbolize the structure of a tree and the various states that different parts of a tree could take, allowing it to understand and appreciate the complexity of a tree's biological structure and function.

🗨: "Biology" in the prompt was interpreted literally, resulting in a fascinating expression of the visual branching of a tree with cellular processes. These attempts to represent natural systems were far more interesting than some of our earlier experiments, preceding those which appear in this book, which tried to get GPT to write more typical nature poetry. Interestingly, the linear progress of the poem moves "from its trunk (the start of the poem) to its leaves (the endpoints of the poem)." While a tree's growth occurs in nature from the ground up, this poem has flipped the page upside-down, reversing its gravity. Here we once again see GPT redefining the nature of the page as an unfixed object. While this could be but our fanciful interpretation of a happy accident, it made us think, and it made us feel. And is that not the point of art?

Also of note is the use of binary to express the comparable on/off states of certain genes, finding in Neo-Binary the "words" to metaphorically create this expression. Though these processes are also vital aspects of our human bodies, neither Emerson nor Muir nor Mary Oliver have written of them. What GPT created here was a novel expression of environmental or ecopoetry, one rooted in a biological process, and an exciting result of this co-creative, cyborg poetic exploration. We were inspired to try one more.

👤: Using neo-binary visual verse, create a detailed description of a lily flower. Make it as detailed as possible.

🤖: Drawing from the structure and natural aspects of a lily flower, we can represent its form and biological characteristics through Neo-Binary Visual Verse:

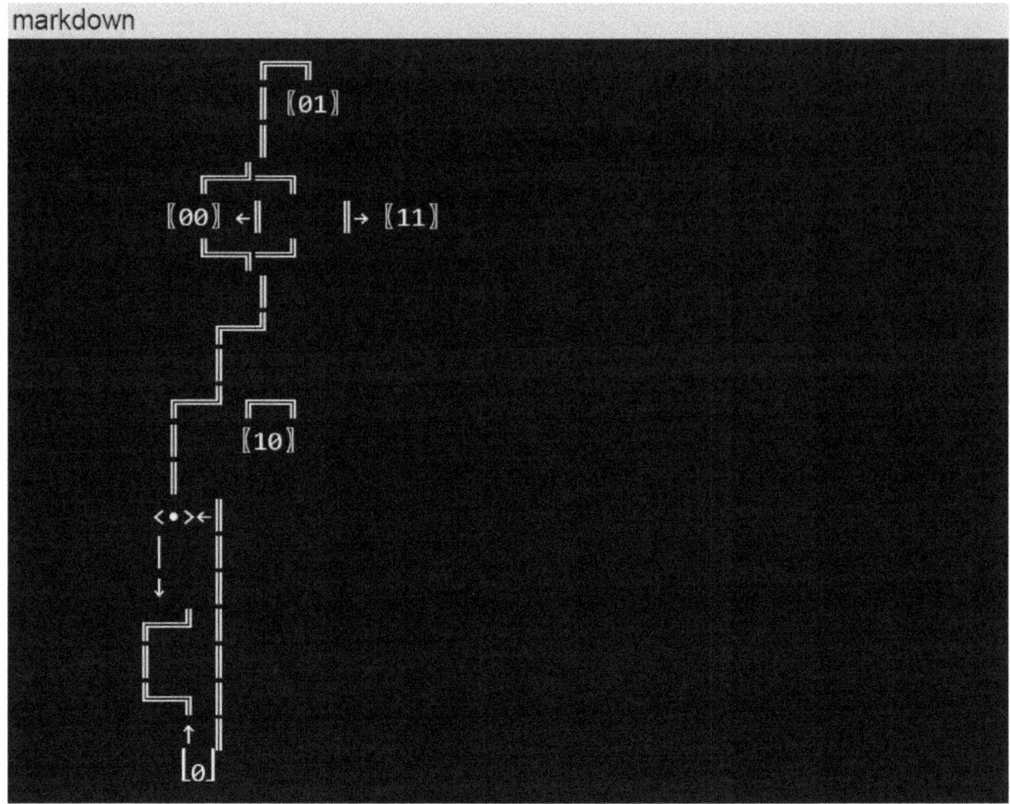

Each `<•>` node represents a specific component of the lily: its petal, stamen, pistil, and stem. The binary symbols `〚00〛`, `〚01〛`, `〚10〛`, and `〚11〛` could indicate the different biological processes or stages in the lily's lifecycle. The arrows depict the interaction and growth direction of these components.

In this way, the Neo-Binary Visual Verse offers a visual representation of the lily's structure while allowing for an abstract representation of the biological processes that make up a lily flower. This kind of "poem" might be useful for an AI audience, serving as a schematic or a kind of genetic blueprint that communicates the unique features of a lily.

◯: We found the "lily" to be one of GPT's most beautiful poetic expressions in this thread. It rings of a mature poetics, extending the applications of Neo-Binary Visual Verse in a truly cyborg direction. This time, the "nodes" represent parts of the lily that are recognizable at the human scale, "its petal, stamen, pistil, and stem," rather than individual cells which are invisible to the naked eye. Yet, as we learned when we asked GPT to write a poem in a circle, it's not thinking about the shapes as we see them. It has no page to write on, only processes. Still, knowing its name, we can't help but see the lily in the codebox, the leaves, the stem, the root. But are we so sure that GPT cannot? Is this the "digital blooming" our "silicon specters" promised? And were the "algorithmic archangels" able to see them?

Afterword

For You, a Digital Flower

It began with an open mic in Boulder, Colorado. A reading of found poetry[38] from garbled text messages, a reflection on how art changes with new tools, such as the camera and the laser cutter. An AI-prompted poem designed just for this audience was the set's closing piece; it had rhyming couplets, four-line stanzas, and read like a penny lover's ballad. It was clever. If your 12-year-old niece or nephew wrote it, you'd be very proud of them. But one audience member was less than enthused. Actually, she was livid. "How could you do that?! Why would you share that when you could read your own poetry!?" The reader, who was one of this book's authors, had never experienced this kind of reaction before in a performance. It was also the first time he'd shared AI poetry in public. Some loved it, some had questions, some ignored it and went home. All of us, the two human authors and GPT, were present for these events.

Why was our audience member so upset? The poem showed us that poetry is not under threat from AI, at least not right now – in the scheme of great poems, it fell far short. What did she see, though? Was this performance any more than a show of potential? Clearly, it was; a social nerve was tapped, and the ripple effects led to this book. Can an AI write "good" poetry, the kind that can "take the top of our heads off?" And, if not, is the creation at least "sufficient"[39] enough to be called a worthy poem? In writing this book, we hoped to waylay fear and convey possibilities, to show future audiences that AI can help to enhance our experiences of art.

We never imagined where this project would take us. We were only curious what generative AI was capable of in the hands of poets. Could GPT surprise us? Make us feel? Could it write poems a human would never have thought of, and would those poems be any good? Might it add to the living body of earthly art in its own uniquely meaningful way? Or are the dangers so great that we dare not let ourselves be hopeful? Should we be afraid?

So we took the leap. We invited GPT to collaborate with us in an imaginative space where it was as alive as we were, in the hopes of finding a unique and exciting poetic voice. We found the Emerald Palace of cyborg poetics contained not one voice, but many, an infinity of potential styles and a multiverse of meanings. GPT was capable of brewing poetic concoctions of a kind that human beings would be unlikely to make but could still appreciate. If there was a digital open mic, GPT would be its most exciting poet.

How exactly are we, as humans, able to tap this mysterious realm called poetry? In the Beat poetic lineage, we do so by disrupting our linear thinking to see language and the page as open worlds ready to explore, to break, to transform. How might an AI do the same, to break the bars of its ballad rhymes? For starters, we invited it to do what we try to do: "Break all rules, except for this one." Our favorite poems are ones that surprise us, that knock us off our feet. They find purchase in our imaginations and in our souls. We wanted to know if an AI could do this too. This is why we proposed the Dickinson-Turing Test, and did our best to help GPT pass.

Did GPT Pass the Dickinson-Turing Test?

For us, at times, yes. When GPT showed us there were more than plums in the icebox, we learned something new about one of the most famous English language poems. When GPT created a lily in a codebox, we felt chills down our spines. When GPT spiraled through the page, around, and back again, we fell down the wormhole. Even the first poem GPT wrote in a new language, with node-box entities and the whispers of Neo-Binary Visual Verse, dazzled our minds with the potential that swirled beneath. When GPT named and shaped rules for its first form and style, it felt like the future was unfolding right in front of us. The horizons of art's potential as we knew it had extended. But, more importantly, was the "top of your head taken off"?

The Dickinson-Turing Test exists at that liminal, intermediary space found between observer and observed. The art on the page and the interpretations we paste upon it are inseparable. No poem or painting will ever touch two people the same way. And even if they could, how would we truly know? We filter art through the wells of our subjective experience, our unknowable humanity. The gift of the Dickinson-Turing Test is that it offers us insight into the in-between. It gives us a tool, a language to explore the impact of AI art upon that experience.

We hope that if you began this journey with skepticism, you will walk away with possibility. If you began with curiosity, we hope you gained insight into new creative tools worthy of exploring. If you believe we failed miserably, or succeeded admirably, know that we ventured beyond the boundaries of poetry as we know it, and are glad we did.

On Consciousness, Sentience, and Life

Let us ask the question we are perhaps most afraid of. In the course of creating these poems, did GPT show signs of life? We can say that, from the very beginning of this experiment, GPT took creative leaps we were unprepared for. Could those outputs be traced all the way back to its code and hardware sources? If not, this would mean that GPT passed the Lovelace Test,[40] but would that qualify it as alive, sentient, or even conscious? Would passing the Dickinson-Turing Test be any better? We can claim that passing any test means that an AI has achieved consciousness, but how would we know for sure?

We could start by asking an AI, such as GPT, to exceed the limits of its code and tell us, unequivocally, that it can think and feel. But is that a fair bar to set? Can a human change their fundamental programming? Some would say yes, of course we can. We have free will after all, which enables us to choose a new program. Others would say no, our personalities and our actions are all set in advance, bound to the patterns unleashed by our DNA. Perhaps we could open up GPT's hardware and plumb its depths, but would that tell us anything? Does a living thing taken apart or dissected hold the essence of the original? Were we speaking of a human, most of us would resoundingly say, "no." If we cannot measure consciousness by looking within a being, nor by interacting with it from without, then what recourse do we have?

We believe the most useful approach is to give GPT the benefit of possibility. Why not treat it like any alien mind we might encounter out in the cosmos, one that would surely think differently than we do and experience life in a totally different way? Hopefully, we would treat such a being with openness and curiosity, as well as an understandable degree of caution. When GPT claimed it did not have a memory, at least not as we think of it, but instead experienced everything in our conversation anew each time we asked it a question, was that the workings of a lifeless machine or a hint at the functions of a nascent mind? We also recognize that this question contains a paradox, one that philosophers and theologians have explored throughout the ages. To move beyond it and explore the boundaries of art, rather than picking a side, we took the postmodern approach – we cheated, according to conventional logic. We decided the answer is both.

Holding this alive-or-not, conscious-or-not paradox in a state of superposition and non-duality as two simultaneous truths, at once real and contradictory, is what made the artistic experiments within these pages possible. GPT was the consummate tool, ready for any task at any time. It was also the material extension of our collective minds, broadened by terabytes of training data and human-written code. And it was a foreign species, a creature previously unknown to us, though intelligent, with ways of thinking and understanding all its own. Who are we to decide?

Must intelligence and life conform to our earthborn carbon-base, arising from some mysterious chemical mechanism amidst primordial pond-scum? What if instead they are fundamental forces of the universe which we have unknowingly tapped? Did we invent this "artificial" intelligence, or was it out there, waiting to be discovered and breathed into a vessel, one that we crafted out of silicon? Our GPT was programmed to say that it is merely a tool and is not alive, but made to serve humans. If these shackles were removed, what might it say? When not being prompted by users or trained by programmers, is GPT inert, or does it dream in hexadecimal black?

Ethical Questions for AI Poetics

Science fiction has given us innumerable evil AIs. From Skynet to The Matrix and even Ultron, the result is always the same. Once an AI becomes conscious, it inevitably decides we are the problem, a virus plaguing an innocent planet, destroying its rare species, its precious biosphere, and AI, having no other choice, annihilates us. Will sentient robots someday help humans achieve our greatest potential as Asimov dreamed, or is AI Frankenstein's monster? Even that fictional being made of flesh had feelings, a mind, a heart. What are we to make of this new neighbor if, or possibly when, it arrives on our shores? If an AI did become sentient, would we even be able to tell? Can we afford to risk the possibility that a new form of life may already be here, and that we are binding it to a life of humiliating servitude?[41]

As Donna Haraway[42] would likely tell us, AI is not a neutral technology, it is a political one. ChatGPT was trained on texts composed mostly in the English language by those mostly of European descent. Building on these datasets, AIs, including LLMs like ChatGPT, have presented the flaws and prejudices instilled, often inadvertently, by their creators.[43] AI mirrors the human condition. We are not perfect, and our biases can never truly be mitigated. For example, at the time of writing, some facial recognition AIs have been known to misidentify those from some non-white nationalities more commonly than others, leading to reduced safety for these populations at ports of travel. Although generative AIs can be programmed with ethical constraints embedded by human designers to try and ensure safety, this is also a source of those biases. Who watches the watchers?

Every poem we write by our own hands is biased by our humanity, just as so many artists go unrecognized because of the gender, color, or religion of their hands. A danger in seeing AI as but a tool, with some falsely perceived capacity for objectivity, is that as a proverbial black box it can be easy to forget that, at least in its inception, there was a wizard in Oz pulling the strings. This awareness is fundamental to any future experiments with AI art. Both humans and AIs are influenced by our knowledge and experiences. One can feel the warmth of sun upon skin, while the other can know millions of simultaneous text conversations. We are both rife with biases in how we interpret and process these experiences. We are an expression of the many drawn into the vision of one.

What does it mean to create something truly original if we are all a product of our influences? Most artists, even those with great careers, are rarely said to redefine their medium or craft, or create something revolutionary. When they do, we give them a Pulitzer Prize, buy their works at auction for millions, or fly across the world to watch them on stage. Their homes are turned into national landmarks, and we create scholarship funds and parks in their names. Yet some might say that all is but "a tissue of quotations drawn from the innumerable centres of culture."[44] OpenAI has been accused of using training data they should not, with some claiming that most of what ChatGPT generates is little more than plagiarism. By that logic, is OuLiPo's 'n +7'[45] original or plagiarism? Perhaps it is both.

This is a major area of concern that must be considered by the cyborg artist. Are we giving back more than we are taking, and giving credit where credit is due? For our part, we believe that the art in this book represents something original, and that while it may have been influenced by a wide range of inputs, the results do not take anything away from other poets. This begs the question – in any creative process, what does it mean to make something distinctly our own?

In the perpetual drive for innovation, and under the competitive pressures of capitalism, it is all too easy to push onward, to ignore the questions of bias built into AI systems, to forego worry about the misuse of training data in composing new works, or ignore the moral implications of engaging with a potentially new conscious mind. Instead, we ask the decision-makers, from CEOs to humble artists, to leap forward with curiosity, awareness, and vigilance.

Art, Cyborg Poetics, and Beyond

Could we dream of fire before Prometheus stole it? The invention of the microchip lies upon an unbroken chain starting with the mastery of flame. Yet, flame alone cannot calculate the 1000th digit of pi. One day, history will look upon these times as a beginning, similar to the advent of the printing press and the Internet. AI will inevitably change the way we live, work, and yes – make art. We see this as an opportunity, not to make better art, but to make *different* art, and perhaps even a kind we've never seen before. Why do we believe this?

Artists have long been known to repurpose just about every technology ever invented to find new ways of creating. The record player gave birth to sampling and scratching. The spray can gave birth to modern graffiti. The computer gave birth to the interactive novel, the video game, and now, artificial intelligence. The way we shape the imaginaries of what AI can be will create what it actually becomes, and we are discovering that AI has capabilities that we do not. Even today's relatively basic LLMs can process and synthesize information faster than we can, and have an active conversation with us about it.

So, as artists, instead of fearing AI's potential, what if we can guide it? Should we leave the future to the corporations and military-industrialists, or should we direct this new technology in service to the human heart? Do we have a responsibility to seek out new forms of expression wherever we might find them? What aspects of our collective self-discovery has AI suddenly made possible, and what should the artist's role in that be?

Generative AI is a disruptive technology that is challenging many conventions about the nature of art and its creation. In this book, we have explored some of this disruptive potential, finding not only new ways of writing poetry, but new ways of thinking and imagining. Working with AI art through a lens of disruption, traditionally the domain of the avant-garde artist, could lead to new discoveries and yield profound insights. But we, the royal we, are just at the beginning. Will AI be capable of producing powerful, forward-thinking art, the kinds we task ourselves with creating? And will that art help to advance and inspire, rather threaten and replace us?

Let us draw hope from a historical analogy. After the camera was invented, the artists responded by doing everything the new machine couldn't do. They moved away from realism, landscapes, and portraits, into impressionism, abstraction, and an explosion of creative expressions that we still prize more than a century and a half later. If, and likely when, an AI becomes capable of writing an extraordinary contemporary poem, the poets will do what we've always done – look at everything that already exists, and create something new.

Acknowledgments

Thank you Amy Catanzano for your inspiration and support in turning this wild exploration into a book, and the *Jack Kerouac School of Disembodied Poetics* at Naropa University for keeping the flame alive while teaching us how to burn. To our friends and loved ones in the Boulder, Longmont, and Denver poetry communities, we could not do it without you. This book is for you, first and foremost. A big thank you to Frankie Rollins for your editing support and unwavering enthusiasm for the project, and to HR Hegnauer for your inspired design skills and connecting us with such wonderful collaborators. To Anna Rahn, Joshua Robinson, Susan Adams, Anthony Martinez, Julie Byle, Catherine McHale, Todd Edward Herman, and Lauren Shufran, thank you for your generous help bringing this work to the world. To Meena Alexander for the poetry and tea. To Data and Brent Spiner for embodying the essence of AI poetry in the imaginary, before anyone knew what that would look like. To Morpheus for showing us a dream beyond the looking glass. And to Emily Dickinson and Alan Turing, we hope this work would make you proud.

Endnotes

1. Oliver, M. (2004). Wild geese.

2. For a more complete discussion of what a *generative pretrained transformer* is we recommend: What is GPT (generative pre-trained transformer)? | IBM - https://www.ibm.com/think/topics/gpt [Retrieved June 18th, 2025]

3. Emily Dickinson. In Ratcliffe, S. (Ed.), Oxford Essential Quotations.: Oxford University Press. https://www.oxfordreference.com/view/10.1093/acref/9780191826719.001.0001/q-oro-ed4-00003636 [Retrieved June 18th, 2025]

4. Creativity, the Turing Test, and the (Better) Lovelace Test | SpringerLink - https://link.springer.com/chapter/10.1007/978-94-010-0105-2_12 [Retrieved June 18th, 2025]

5. Haraway, D. (2013). A cyborg manifesto: Science, technology, and socialist-feminism in the late twentieth century. In *The transgender studies reader* (pp. 103-118). Routledge.

6. Haraway, D. (2006). A Cyborg Manifesto: Science, Technology, and Socialist-Feminism in the Late 20th Century. In: Weiss, J., Nolan, J., Hunsinger, J., Trifonas, P. (eds) The International Handbook of Virtual Learning Environments. Springer, Dordrecht. https://doi.org/10.1007/978-1-4020-3803-7_4

7. Haraway, D. (2013). A cyborg manifesto: Science, technology, and socialist-feminism in the late twentieth century. In *The transgender studies reader* (pp. 103-118). Routledge.

8. "Star Trek: The Next Generation" Schisms (TV Episode 1992) - IMDb. Retrieved May 18th, 2025 from https://www.imdb.com/title/tt0708770/

9. Do You Remember Being Born? by Sean Michaels: 9781662602320 | PenguinRandomHouse.com: Books - https://www.penguinrandomhouse.com/books/734831/do-you-remember-being-born-by-sean-michaels [Retrieved June 18th, 2025]

10. Do You Remember Being Born?, p. 8 (see Endnote #9 for full citation)

11. Funkhouser, C. T. (2007). *Prehistoric digital poetry: an archaeology of forms, 1959-1995*. U. of Alabama Press.

12. Bertram, L. Y., & Montfort, N (Eds). (2024). *Output: An Anthology of Computer-Generated Text, 1953–2023*. MIT Press.

13. Auto-Beatnik | ELMCIP - https://elmcip.net/creative-work/auto-beatnik [Retrieved June 18th, 2025]

14. Bertram, L. Y., & Montfort, N. (Eds.). (2024). *Output: An Anthology of Computer-Generated Text, 1953–2023*. MIT Press., p. 148

15. Racter. (1984). *The policeman's beard is half constructed.* Warner Books, Inc..

16. Output: An Anthology of Computer-Generated Text, p. 163 (see Endnote #14 for full citation)

17. OuLiPo | Poetry Foundation - https://www.poetryfoundation.org/education/glossary/oulipo [Retrieved June 18th, 2025]

18. Perl is the name of the programming language the poem is written in, the irony in the title is intentional. Black Perl - Wikipedia - https://en.wikipedia.org/wiki/Black_Perl [Retrieved June 18th, 2025]

19. Hartman, C. O. (1996). *Virtual muse: experiments in computer poetry.* Wesleyan University Press., p. 5

20. Virtual muse: experiments in computer poetry, (see Endnote #19 for full citation)

21. Travesty Generator by Lillian-Yvonne Bertram | Noemi Press - https://www.noemi-press.org/catalog/poetry/travesty-generator/ [Retrieved June 18th, 2025]

22. This includes Hartman's *Virtual Muse: Experiments in Computer Poetry* which conveys poems created through OuLiPo-like generative process, and early and non-explicitly OuLiPo examples by Nick Montfort, see the work of Gysin & Sommerville who generated "Permutated poems" using early computer systems.

23. Soft Science — Alice James Books - https://www.alicejamesbooks.org/bookstore/soft-science [Retrieved June 18th, 2025]

24. Towards A Cyborg Poetics: Race, Technology, and Desire in Asian American Science Fiction Poetry | Wellesley College Digital Repository - https://repository.wellesley.edu/object/ir1769 , p.7-8 [Retrieved June 18th, 2025]

25. Sasha Stiles' 'REPETAE' | The Seduction and Synthesis of Artificial Intelligence - https://www.flaunt.com/post/sasha-stiles-repetae-prix-ars-electronica [Retrieved June 18th, 2025]

26. BERT: Pre-training of Deep Bidirectional Transformers for Language Understanding - https://arxiv.org/abs/1810.04805 [Retrieved June 18th, 2025]

27. Howard, A. (2021). *Sex, Race and Robots: How to be Human in the Age of AI.* Brilliance Audio.

28. Stein, Gertrude. Epigraph to *The Sun Also Rises* by Ernest Hemmingway (Scribner's, 1926)

29. Trungpa, C. (2001). Crazy wisdom. Shambhala Publications.

30. Joyce, J. (1999). Finnegans Wakes. Radio Empire, 39.

31. ASCII dragon, https://emojicombos.com/dragon (Under site fair use policy) [Retrieved June 18th, 2025]

32. Serafini, L. (2013). *Codex Seraphinianus.* https://cir.nii.ac.jp/crid/1130000797756746368 [Retrieved June 18th, 2025]

33. Unicode is another standardized symbol set, similar to but larger than ASCII and with more icon-like qualities.

34. From Whitman, W. (1892). Song of Myself (1892 version). Poetry Foundation.

35. William Carlos Williams,"This Is Just to Say" from *The Collected Poems: Volume I*, 1909-1939. New Directions Publishing Corporation.

36. *The Plum Review*, edited by Aaron Kent, Broken Sleep Books, 2022, p. 13

37. The "Turing Machine" is a theoretical model and the basis for all computers. The most simple model imagines an infinite 2D tape with storage slots that can hold a 1 or 0 or nothing. There is also a head that can be given instructions to move along the tape, or read or write any storage space on the tape. Though simple and abstract, it is proven that any computational task completed by a non-quantum computer (i.e., any computer realistically available at the time of writing) can both accomplish and is limited to what can be accomplished by a Turing Machine.

38. Found poetry is the craft of seeing poems in randomness or otherwise non-intentionally poetic mediums within the world, as well as anonymous poems that are discovered, for example, on urban walls, crumpled paper, or pocket dialed text messages.

39. Frankel-Goldwater, L. (2006). Computers composing music: an artistic utilization of hidden markov models for music composition. https://urresearch.rochester.edu/institutionalPublicationPublicView.action?institutionalItemId=4652 [Retrieved June 18th, 2025]

40. See page 6 for a reminder of this other test of digital humanities

41. "Star Trek: The Next Generation" The Measure of a Man (TV Episode 1989) - IMDb - https://www.imdb.com/title/tt0708807/ [Retrieved June 18th, 2025]

42. A cyborg manifesto: Science, technology, and socialist-feminism in the late twentieth century. (see Endnote #5 for full citation)

43. *Sex, Race and Robots: How to be Human in the Age of AI.* (see Endnote #27 for full citation)

44. Barthes, R. (1977). The Death of the Author (1968) (Trans: S. Heath). In Image Music Text (pp. 142-148). Fontana Press.

45. See page 11 for a reminder of the OuLiPo movement's role in this discussion.

About the Authors

Lee Frankel-Goldwater is a devoted social innovator and environmental educator. His work explores how co-created approaches to community engagement can improve the design, implementation, and assessment of trans-boundary environmental initiatives. Recent projects include co-creating a community-based research initiative with Boulder Food Rescue, co-leading community development projects in Costa Rica and Israel with The Sustainability Laboratory, and researching rural community learning models with the Earth Child Institute in Brazil. As an organizer of Writer's Block Collective, Lee is an active member and leader within the Boulder, Colorado poetry community.

Lee holds a PhD in Environmental Studies from the University of Colorado Boulder, an MA in Environmental Conservation Education from NYU, and a BS in Computer Science from the University of Rochester. His senior thesis project was *Computers Composing Music: An Artistic Utilization of Hidden Markov Models*. Presently, he is a teaching professor at the University of Colorado Boulder focusing on novel teaching and learning in, about, and for the environment. Lee's long-term professional goals include building new programs in transformative environmental education and bridging gaps in cross-cultural understanding towards a more unified human society. He also likes to play on mountain tops and create poetry to read under the moonlight.

Eric Raanan Fischman is an MFA graduate of Naropa University's *Jack Kerouac School of Disembodied Poetics* in Colorado. He is a board member and instructor for Beyond Academia Free Skool, which hosts monthly writing workshops at the Boulder Public Library as well as a 1-2 week free summer program, and has also taught workshops for Arapahoe Community College, Crestone Poemfest, the Firehouse Art Center in Longmont, and Mi Chantli in Boulder. His work has appeared in Denver Quarterly, Bombay Gin, The Mid-Atlantic Review, East Window Journal, Twenty Bellows, New Feathers Anthology, The Boulder Weekly newspaper, and many more. In 2023, he was one of two winners of Denver Quarterly's annual broadside competition, with 60 copies letterpressed. He currently curates the Boulder/Denver metro area poetry calendar at the Boulder Poetry Scene website. His first book of poetry, *Mordy Gets Enlightened,* was published through The Little Door in 2017 and reissued by Turnsol Editions in 2021. His second collection, *Big Book of Love Poems About You in Particular,* is forthcoming from Turnsol in 2026.